Every Story Starts with Small Steps: Avondale COVID-19 Journal is a vulnerable, heartwarming, and sometimes heartbreaking glimpse into the experiences of a school community during the COVID-19 global pandemic. Karen weaves the stories seamlessly together, telling them with grace and compassion. Everyone who reads it will be able to relate to something in this book and will feel more connected and validated in their own experiences.

—Kristina Black Avondale Elementary Principal

I was a high school math teacher for nine years before leaving school to become a parent and pursue a competitive curling career as an athlete then as a national team coach. During the COVID-19 pandemic, there were many days when I wondered how I would have handled my kids— your students are always your kids—and continued to educate while helping them navigate the unknown. Karen's narrative is genuine and insightful. The honesty and vulnerability capture the ebb and flow of educators during the pandemic. And they are real people with families and worries of their own. In reading *Every Story Starts with Small Steps*, I felt connected to my community, and many of the stories resonated with me. At the end of a time of isolation, I feel less alone in my experience and find hope in these words. Thank you, Karen, for reminding me how incredible humanity is.

—Rene Sonnenberg
National Curling Canada
Team Coach

Christmas
2021
from Wendy

EVERY

Story

STARTS

WITH SMALL

STEPS

Avondale Elementary
COVID-19 Journal

Karen Powell

Printed in Canada

ISBN: 978-1-4866-2208-5
eBook ISBN: 978-1-4866-2209-2

Word Alive Press
119 De Baets Street Winnipeg, MB R2J 3R9
www.wordalivepress.ca

Cataloguing in Publication information can be obtained from Library and Archives Canada.

Christmas 2021
Love
Wendy & Dwane

To my
2019/20 and 2020/21
Avondale Elementary Family

*Let Your work appear to Your servants, and Your glory
to their children. And let the beauty of the Lord God be
upon us, And establish the work of our hands for us;
Yes, establish the work of our hands.*
(Psalm 90:16-17)

Acknowledgements

History: The study of past events. The whole series of events connected with someone or something. Though my high school History teacher extolled the virtues of studying history, I didn't appreciate then how significantly the past impacts the future. Nor did I fully understand and connect with my part—every day I wake up, and with each step that I take, I am creating history. When I own this privilege and responsibility, I respond with more intentionality and purpose: first, always try to be kind. Second, to record and learn from history as I journal my response to COVID-19. And third, to share and honour the experiences of Avondale School, the place where I work as an Educational Assistant.

The coronavirus pandemic was one of many major crises in 2020–2021. Though my journal focuses primarily on the impact of COVID-19, other events also influenced my feelings and thoughts. What seemed apparent, everywhere and in every situation, was the need for, and the power of, empathy, connection, and community.

Health problems and the duration, threat, and restrictions of COVID-19 all contributed to periods where I felt fearful, low, and isolated. While writing Part Three, I acknowledged my experiences honestly and as legitimately challenging. I recognized that the way through was a thankful heart, connection, and perspective. I saw the whole picture. A beautiful life. Intricate jewels painstakingly placed. My experiences, though uniquely mine, are what connects me to others. My history, and my present, include many loving and supportive relationships and communities for which I am very grateful. Ups and downs, and twists and turns, have shaped me and led me to the warm and welcoming community of Avondale School.

To my Avondale School family—those I work with and care for—students and staff: Your genuine, determined, and caring hearts and attitude are touching and inspiring. Walking alongside each of you as we journeyed into the unknown was/is a comfort and a pleasure. Thank you for your support and for trusting me with your thoughts, feelings, and heartfelt expressions.

Thank you to my dear friends Stacy Quinn and Cheri Troyer. Your honesty and encouragement bolstered my courage and affirmed the value, authenticity, and vulnerability of our combined and individual stories, and that they would interest readers.

Thank you to school Principal Kristina Black and those who contributed to the Go-Fund-Me publishing campaign she created. I am humbled and grateful for this incredibly generous gift. It truly speaks to how empathy and community empower, inspire, and transform lives. From the moment I first approached Kristina with my idea to journal, she wholeheartedly embraced it. Her love and acceptance of others is a beautiful quality that ripples throughout our entire staff and students.

Thank you to Jenna Quinn (nine/ten-year-old) for providing me with a student's perspective. Her first journal entry captured the shock and tone of the early days of the COVID-19 pandemic. Her second entry was full of gratitude to be back in school despite all the restrictions. Jenna, keep writing; your voice is important. Thank you for allowing me to share your lovely heart that speaks so clearly through your writing.

Thank you for the writing contributions of Ray Buziak (Teacher) and Phyllis Cash (Educational Assistant).

Thank you to my volunteer editors.

Part One: Pastor Kim Penny, I am thankful for your generosity, diligence, and expertise.

Part Two: Principal and dear friend, Kristina Black, thank you so much for all you have done to support me throughout each step. You are a precious gem!

Part Three: My dear friend, Pauline Wendt. I am very thankful for your brave and beautiful heart. Your faith, love, and friendship move and encourage me always. Your courage and support, editing skills and gift of insight enhanced my writing and helped to clarify my thoughts and feelings as I processed.

Thank you to the two inspirational women who endorsed my writing, who I respect and admire. They share similar traits and perspectives; humble, kind-hearted, and not deterred by large obstacles. They face challenges with optimism and are determined to succeed in the goals they set for themselves. In addition, both women demonstrate a genuine fondness for others and love children.

Kristina Black is a wonderful Principal and leader who encourages and models the Seven Sacred teachings of Avondale: Love, Respect, Courage, Honesty, Wisdom, Humility, and Truth.

Rene Sonnenberg is a fierce competitor in sport and life. However, her fierceness is not directed at the opposition; instead, the desire and grit to do her best and bring out the best in others.

Thank you to family and friends outside of Avondale School. I am so happy to be able to share this experience and am grateful for each of you.

Thank you to Word Alive Press for your support and to Braun Book Awards for Longlisting my manuscript. It is a great honour.

To my Father, in heaven, hallowed be Your name, Your kingdom come, Your will be done, on earth as it is in heaven. (Matthew 6:9-10, NIV).

Introduction

When the coronavirus all started it was in China far away from here, but before we knew it, it got out of China! It got to Italy then Texas. It got closer and closer, and before we knew it, it got to Calgary, then Edmonton: now it *was* in Alberta, where I live. Edmonton started at two cases then four, six, eight, ten, twelve, and sooner than I knew it got to one hundred. Now we were in the state of *emergency*. One day it got to this… Grandma and Grandpa called. They sed school just ended, hay, my mom did not know, then she was like, "No way!" My mom works at a school, and she was shocked. At the time, me and my brother were having spring break where we were downstairs playing. I went upstairs to talk to my mom when she told me schools are out for the rest of the year. I got sad and started to cry. I ran downstairs to tell my brother. One week later my teacher sent me home school homework. Ever since I have been writing in my journal, and I still have more to my story. I miss my teachers and friends and also a normal life. I have so much planned for when this is over or when the third wave is over at least. I have heard about the 1918 pandemic, and now I am living through the 2020 pandemic and *I don't like it at all!* I can not wait until this is all over.

—Jenna Quinn, Grade 3

World Heath Organization Director-General's opening remarks at the media briefing on COVID-19 — March 11, 2020:
Good afternoon,

In the past two weeks, the number of cases of COVID-19 outside China has increased 13-fold, and the number of affected countries has tripled. There are now more than 118,000 cases in 114 countries, and 4,291 people have lost their lives. Thousands more are fighting for their lives in hospitals. In the days and weeks ahead, we expect to see the number of cases, the number of deaths, and the number of affected countries climb even higher. WHO has been assessing this outbreak around the clock and we are deeply concerned both by the alarming levels of spread and severity, and by the alarming levels of inaction. We have therefore made the assessment that COVID-19 can be characterized as a Pandemic. Pandemic is not a word to use lightly or carelessly. It is a word that, if misused, can cause unreasonable fear, or unjustified acceptance that the fight is over, leading to unnecessary suffering and death. Describing the situation as a pandemic does not change WHO's assessment of the threat posed by this virus. It doesn't change what WHO is doing, and it doesn't change what countries should do. We have never before seen a pandemic sparked by a coronavirus. This is the first pandemic caused by a coronavirus. And we have never before seen a pandemic that can be controlled, at the same time. WHO has been in full response mode since we were notified of the first cases. And we have called every day for countries to take urgent and aggressive action. We have rung the alarm bell loud and clear.

As I said on Monday, just looking at the number of cases and the number of countries affected does not tell the full story. Of the 118,000 cases reported globally in 114 countries, more than 90 percent of cases are in just four countries, and two of those – China and the Republic of Korea — have significantly declining epidemics.

81 countries have not reported any cases, and 57 countries have reported 10 cases or less.

We cannot say this loudly enough, or clearly enough, or often enough: all countries can still change the course of this pandemic.

If countries detect, test, treat, isolate, trace, and mobilize their people in response, those with a handful of cases can prevent those cases becoming clusters, and those clusters becoming community transmission. Even those countries with community transmission or large clusters can turn the tide on this virus. Several countries have demonstrated that this virus can be suppressed and controlled. The challenge for many countries who are now dealing with large clusters or community transmission is not whether they can do the same — it's whether they will. Some countries are struggling with a lack of capacity. Some countries are struggling with a lack of resources. Some countries are struggling with a lack of resolve. We are grateful for the measures being taken in Iran, Italy and the Republic of Korea to slow the virus and control their epidemics. We know that these measures are taking a heavy toll on societies and economies, just as they did in China. All countries must strike a fine balance between protecting health, minimizing economic and social disruption, and respecting human rights. WHO's mandate is public health. But we're working with many partners across all sectors to mitigate the social and economic consequences of this pandemic. This is not just a public health crisis; it is a crisis that will touch every sector — so every sector and every individual must be involved in the fight. I have said from the beginning that countries must take a whole-of-government, whole-of-society approach, built around a comprehensive strategy to prevent infections, save lives and minimize impact. Let me summarize it in four key areas. First, prepare and be ready. Second, detect, protect and treat. Third, reduce transmission. Fourth, innovate and learn. I remind all countries that we are calling on you to activate and scale up your emergency response mechanisms; Communicate with your people about the risks and how they can protect themselves — this is everybody's business; Find, isolate, test and treat every case and trace every contact; Ready your hospitals; Protect and train your health workers. And let's all look out for each other, because we need each other.

There's been so much attention on one word. Let me give you some other words that matter much more, and that are much more actionable. Prevention. Preparedness. Public health. Political leadership. And most of all, people. We're in this together, to do the right things with calm and protect the citizens of the world. It's doable. I thank you.

We were alarmed when Alberta's cases jumped from seven to fourteen.

On March 16, the province of Alberta ordered all daycares to close, all K-12 schools to suspend classes, and all post-secondary institutions to switch to online classes. Grade 12 diploma exams would still occur.

On March 17, Premier Kenny declared a state of emergency for Alberta.

The first wave peaked on April 30, when the number of active cases of COVID-19 in the province reached 3,022.

Hinshaw said at her March 18 update, "We have had to weigh lives against livelihoods. And in order to save lives, I have had to make recommendations that will take away livelihoods from many Albertans over the next several weeks to months. There are no easy solutions to the situation we are in, not only in Alberta but around the world."

On March 19, Hinshaw announced the first death in Alberta.

On June 15, the provincial state of emergency ended.

On June 16, the province reported thirty-five new cases and 449 active cases. A petition by Alberta doctors calling on government officials to make wearing a mask mandatory in indoor public spaces was circulating.

In the early weeks of the COVID-19 global pandemic, I had an inspired moment to invite my coworkers to join me in a project: to journal the remainder of the 2019/2020 school year. How is the coronavirus impacting us personally and professionally? Journaling helps me to express and process my thoughts and feelings. It creates clarity and order. I needed to find a way to feel purposeful. Perhaps, I could help my coworkers clarify their thoughts and feelings too.

Dear Staff,

I would like to propose and engage our Staff in an endeavour— to Journal our school's response to the pandemic. Describe what this crisis looked and felt like through the lens of educators. Admittedly, this Novel Coronavirus is a scary opponent. It is a harmful and unpredictable virus that is limiting, isolating, and persistent as it stalks every corner of the earth. It is impossible to change the facts. What if, together, we transform the narrative of COVID-19 as it applies to our school, collectively and individually? We embrace the challenge, determined to overcome the obstacles and anxiety that we are sure to face. Let's build and focus on what we know to be good, lovely, and hopeful.

My hope is to meet with each staff member willing to share their thoughts and experiences thus far. I want to highlight and record both challenges and victories. Capture humanness. Emotions. Togetherness. Aloneness. Whatever comes. This means asking questions and keeping informed. It means a certain level of vulnerability and trust. Understand, whatever you choose to share with me, I will only share what you are comfortable with. My thoughts and outline are not well-formed just yet, and I'm open to suggestions.

Thoughts to consider: What was the undercurrent of emotion the last day we had students in the school? What were you feeling? What about your students, how was their behaviour? What were some of their questions and concerns? What did it feel like returning to empty classrooms? To remember to stay two metres away from one another? How overwhelming was the task of contacting parents, rounding up students' belongings and preparing a week's worth of work for them? How much pressure was there to learn new online programs quickly? How did you encourage one another? What personal concerns for yourself and your family did you have? Health, well-being and financial security.

Future weeks will be examined and measured, celebrated or resigned. What we do today won't just impact the next few weeks or months (but will inform a new protocol for responding to an educational crisis). What we are doing is pioneering! History teaches us that pioneering is not an easy life. It requires hard work and a close-knit community. Brave, adventurous souls.

Thanks, Karen.

Brave is not a reckless or caution-less action or response. The dictionary says of 'brave': ready to face and suffer danger or pain, to endure or face unpleasant conditions or behaviour without showing fear, having or showing mental or moral strength to face danger, fear or difficulty: having or showing courage. Synonyms for brave: bold, courageous, dauntless, fearless, gallant, gutsy, heroic, lionhearted, stalwart, valiant.

I would add of bravery, that it acts wisely and out of necessity. It is a choice, and it's impossible to measure or judge another's amount of courage. Disillusioned pioneers realized that the risk of returning from whence they came was often as perilous and dangerous as the hardships in front of them. Without proper protection and resources, they would surely fail. Their best option was to work together. To put ingenuity to work. Accept where they were. The present. Make the best out of what they had.

Society is unaccustomed to being hampered and limited in their movements. How can we best serve our children? Protect them and ourselves.? Not just from contracting COVID, but more so, from all the ways COVID has impacted their/our day-to-day lives. I believe we will find opportunities to teach more than just letters and numbers. For the last few years, there has been a tremendous effort to foster empathy in our society, especially in our schools. Facebook (social media) posts uplifting quotes. We do not lack inspirational stories. Words. Words are wonderful, but they mean nothing without action. Without genuine feeling and caring. Our kids have a chance to truly be immersed in empathy. Their actions shape the future. Seldom does loving well come without sacrifice. Wearing a mask, keeping our distance, washing our hands, staying home when sick, trying our best to look out for those we love, those we work with or go to school with, even those we have never met. It is a huge responsibility. Responsibility is a privilege. If we, the adults in our children's lives, model, and dare I say, embrace this time in history, so too will they. We have the power to enlighten a generation. Awaken and empower them to be the change. One step at a time. One action. One word. If we each keep taking small steps of bravery and curiosity – imagination – united purpose and support for one another as we move forward and further along the 'New Normal' trail, we can build a highway. Make rough places smooth. Remove the boulders and stones as we come upon them. Pray our hands sustain limited injuries. A few scratches we can surely expect and manage.

Prologue

March 13, 2020

Ten-year-old Justina wrapped her arms tightly around me. It's not out of the ordinary for her, or other children in our school, to reach out to staff for a friendly or encouraging hug. However, this morning there was a different kind of need in her embrace. She leaned in a little longer, her grip firmer. I am skilled at sensing slight nuances in body language and facial expression. She was feeling the same fearful, unexpressed uncertainty the rest of us were feeling. At the end of the hall, a younger child had her arms wrapped around Miss Craig (EA). Mrs. Thomson's (EA) comforting presence encircled another of our students. It's hard to believe that only days later, a national advisory instructed people to keep two metres apart from one another. What will happen to our children who come to school each day seeking consistency, security, and nurture? So much of who I am, and other educators in our school are, is expressed through our touch and reassuring presence.

This week has dismantled our community's false sense of immunity. Two days ago, the WHO declared COVID-19 a worldwide pandemic. And today, at lunch, staff members scoured their phones for information. Alberta now has twenty-nine cases of COVID-19. For the last few weeks, maybe longer, Mrs. Backlund has been sharing with our staff what she's learned about the potential threat of this disease—cautioning us that households should have at least a two-week supply of necessities just in case they had to self-isolate.

Mrs. Backlund (Grace) is very smart, so I wisely heeded her advice. She is not only intelligent but kind and thoughtful. I work as an EA in her classroom, and this morning I found a survival box with my name on it. She waved off my heartfelt thank you. She has a wry sense of humour, "I don't want Ms. Powell to die." Me neither.

At lunchtime, the staff room is buzzing. Several people are giving live updates on the number of COVID-19 cases. Our classrooms are fizzling with heightened unease, expressed in the way children know best—behaviour: noise, distraction, and misinformation. We, the adults, are also anxious. What's going to happen? Yesterday no one was talking about school closures. We acknowledged the possibility—later, if it got closer to us. Now, are we overreacting? Needless panic? Countless people confess they haven't been worried or stockpiling groceries. As humans do, staff members infuse humour into the conversation in an attempt to lighten the atmosphere. Underneath the lighthearted banter, I hear angst.

A quick staff meeting after work reveals Alberta's schools won't be closing, at least not yet. If they close, it will likely be for the rest of the school year. None of us know what to think. Will we see each other on Monday? Is this goodbye for a long time? We are colleagues, yes, but first of all, we are friends. Two years ago, our school was downsized, resulting in subtle, but positive changes in the environment. The smaller size seemed to foster more personal interactions between both staff and students. Though our space decreased, our intentionality increased. We have a clear, united approach to what we do each day. We build relationships. We model our genuine concern, interest, and liking for one another and the students.

Saying goodbye is sombre. Is this really happening?

Part One

March 14

I wonder, *did Grace know she was foreshadowing the future?*

While connecting over the phone, she encouraged, "Go see your grandchildren tomorrow. Hug them and kiss them. It may be a long time before you have another chance." Oh how much I want to go to my daughter's place tomorrow to celebrate my grandsons' combined one and three-year-old birthday party. Last month I missed three days of work with strep throat and ever since hadn't felt very well. A few days after my last dose of penicillin, my throat started to hurt again. At a trip to the doctor earlier this week, he thought my glands were a bit swollen but didn't think I had strep. He wrote out a prescription in case my condition worsened or wasn't better in a week. Today, I am experiencing a sore throat and low-grade fever. Sigh. Hopefully, I will feel better tomorrow.

Grace and I discussed the wisdom of the Minister of Education's decision to continue with classes on Monday. They assured us that proper protocols would be in place. It was absurd. Continuous cleaning amidst a multitude of children, implementing and policing social distancing, and adequate handwashing? This would be a monumental, if not impossible, task.

Later, a friend called for a visit. A mother of two elementary children, she was beside herself that schools were still open. She wouldn't be sending her children to school come Monday. She has an elderly father she was afraid would die if he contracted the virus. After she presented as much evidence as possible to convince me of being careful and safe, she forwarded a post from a friend of a friend currently living in Spain. A dire warning for Canada to heed what was presently happening in Spain and Italy. People in lockdown. Hundreds a day dying. A clear message: don't risk others' health or your own.

March 15

I wish I were feeling better. My family isn't worried whether or not I pass along a bug if I come to the party, but I'm still feeling under the weather, and my friend's conversation and the text she sent were pretty sobering.

Though disappointing, I think it's the right thing to do. I didn't really think I had coronavirus, but still, better safe than sorry; besides, I might have a viral infection of some kind.

My son stopped by after the birthday party for a moment to drop off the prescription of penicillin. The news has us all a little startled. My son was careful and stayed at least six feet away. My head spun. A strange sensation passed in my body as I slid down the wall, whoa. I laughed but was a tiny bit unnerved. I know for certain I won't be going to school tomorrow. "Are you sure you are going to be okay?" my son asked, concerned. I assured him I would be and if I needed anything, I would call him.

This evening, the Minister of Education cancelled Alberta in-school learning for the remainder of the school year. It's official. There is some relief in this. How on earth do schools practice social distancing? There isn't enough space in our classrooms to have desks moved two metres apart. Kids can't keep their hands off each other. One expert said children need ten to twelve touches in an hour. They are continually seeking it—each in their own way. And one or two videos on washing hands, not touching their faces (picking nose), and keeping their hands to themselves isn't going to stick long in their beautiful little minds. Not even in ours. Our hands are gentle, and we use them to comfort and reassure. We have always let our students draw close. We, the adults, use our hands to check in with one another.

Yes, there is some relief in this… but there is also a chilling note of truth: Pandemic. Social distancing. Self-isolating. Self-quarantine. Ventilators. Respirators. ICU. Dying. Many people are dying.

March 15

Alison called to tell me she has lung cancer. It wasn't news I was prepared to hear. There is nothing you can say that seems helpful. Whenever someone shares with me, I try not to jump in but instead listen. Sometimes it is hard—the need to assure or to fix. There is no diminishing how scary cancer is. My family has been through many diagnoses and treatments. I shared one of my family's victories, hope in the face of adversity. It touched me that she had thought to call me. "Is it alright if I pray for you and send you encouraging verses or prayers?" I asked. "Yes, I would appreciate that."

Ms. Alison Mergaert

We have been concerned about Alison for weeks now. She's a funny and dedicated teacher with a sharp wit, keen mind, and soft heart. Of late, her snappy, clever comebacks and observations have been absent from our staff meetings and hallway banter. She has been growing physically tired and discouraged by the lack of a diagnosis and reason for her lethargy. It's only in this last year that I've had the pleasure of getting to know her better. Though we shared mutual respect and appreciation for one another, our paths seldom crossed.

Last summer, while out walking, I saw her mowing her lawn. I stopped, surprised she lived nearby. We greeted one another with a happy hello. She offered me a glass of iced tea in her backyard. It was the first of several. Later that summer, she introduced me to a terrific game: Pickleball! "You will love it!" she passionately declared. "It is addicting." I hesitated at first. And yet, it sounded fun and fit my idea of an excellent way to get exercise. Unlike my friend, I don't readily engage in activities I might not be good at. A week later, I joined her. Her enthusiasm was contagious. Already, she had made friends and had been practicing as much as possible. She encouraged me with every shot. She set up outside matches and introduced the game to two groups of students during Passion Blocks. As for school and COVID, everything coincided with her health leave.

"When I said goodbye to the kids, I had no idea it was going to be goodbye for them too." Due to her serious health concerns, Alison hadn't been following the school news. She was as shocked as the rest of us to learn about school classroom closures. "I can't imagine all the work they (teachers) have had to do," she empathized.

We can't imagine the work she has to do. Alison is a much-loved Avondale girl. Long-standing and new friendships alike are wishing her well, dropping off food and flowers. A birthday drive-by parade of teachers and EAs caught her off guard, touching her heart to the core. She has a small army of women loyal to her in their positive thoughts and care. When asked, "How are you doing?" She shrugs off the hardship. "Not bad. I am grateful and feeling pretty spoiled!"

March 16

Though the school is closed to students, all Grande Prairie Public employees are to be at work today unless they exhibit flu-like symptoms. I have a bit of a struggle. I question my symptoms. I don't have a cough or a runny nose, and I'm not sneezing, the apparent markers for isolating. What am I supposed to do? I slept on and off the last two days, with a sore throat that tested negative for strep throat. We are programmed to push through, especially when our team needs us. My two grandsons' faces come to mind, as well as my mom, a few friends, and a sister-in-law who have compromised immune systems. I don't think I have COVID-19, but what if I do? And what if my pride or flippancy endangers the people I work with? Much as I would like to see them, I know the most responsible thing is to follow the guidelines and stay home.

Later, I talked to several of my coworkers. They, checking up on me, and me, wondering what the day felt like for them. Eery. Quiet. Sombre. Several staff members are away due to illness, and the news that Alison has lung cancer hits everyone hard.

March 16–25

Though I have lived alone for a long time and am comfortable with my own company, self-isolation is surprisingly disconcerting. It is the severity and duration of the restriction. Never has it been deemed dangerous to have a friend or family member inside one's home. A reasonable expectation of a friendly, loving face once enjoyed, is now strongly warned against.

Imposed isolation, along with feeling physically unwell, heightened my sense of vulnerability and unease. This made each act of kindness even more meaningful. My spirit was renewed by family, friends, and coworkers who made sure to stay in contact by text or telephone—at times, merely hearing the care and sound of their voice touched my heart. In response—a tremor in my voice—thankful I am not alone.

Two deliveries of soup were a blessing. Chicken arrived from my friend Shelley and turkey from my aunt Coleen. Between friends, my son, and daughter, my refrigerator has never been packed so full of healthy foods. It seems every few days, a fresh bag of groceries arrives on my doorstep. Stacy (Mrs. Quinn) (EA) provided a laptop from the school to work from home. This allowed video chats with my daughter and grandsons. I am grateful.

Though gratefulness is a helpful attitude to combat negative feelings and circumstances, it doesn't protect one's heart from what the world is currently experiencing. The only measure I can think of that would appear to offer protection is denial, or something more than just physical isolation—emotional isolation. I've lived to some degree in both. It's my place of temptation when overwhelmed with feelings that come too quickly to process. Denial is a poor substitution for connection.

March 25

I'm having a moment of deep sorrow. I had to turn the television off. I turned instead to the radio for comfort or distraction: stories of doctors and nurses who go to work every day and give directives to their coworkers' answers to the worst-case scenario. Refrigerator trucks parked outside of hospitals. Loved ones are dying alone. We are reminded of our complete helplessness and inadequacy to manage this monster. Our best efforts fall far short. My heart is ripped open. I can't imagine the depth of the horror so much of the world is experiencing. Perhaps it is doing a small thing, yet with each small thing we do, we stand with those whose lives are impacted in ways most of us will never know. Breathe... one moment at a time. Do what I can do, and only what I can do. The rest is beyond me, so I must trust in others to do the same. Be effective wherever I am, in whatever capacity. Stay positive. Stay connected. The lessons we will learn if only we keep our hearts open to feel deeply the anguish of others and the beauty of community, kindness, resourcefulness, and servanthood.

March 26

"Oh, Karen, I missed you. It has been a difficult couple of weeks." Grace's (Mrs. Backlund) voice was weary. So much new information to take in and no leeway as to the urgency of deadlines. Grace, like many, is a concerned mother, her two children in need of childcare. Like many, she's a distressed daughter with an elderly mother who lives far away and needs extra care. How could she do both? It's an impossible position—torn; helpless; guilty—There is no way to be enough. My head knew my absence was unavoidable, but an uncomfortable feeling tugged at my heart. I don't feel as though I've been very supportive. We work well together, our space is safe and caring, and our conversations are thoughtful and insightful. Grace has felt alone in her struggles and the daily challenges of this new world. Virtual technology, though a gift, is a cause of great anxiety. I can't imagine the amount of stress and pressure teachers were and are under.

March 28: Day Twelve of Isolation

The last two days, I've started to feel better. I think the physical symptoms that remain are emotionally based. My calm, accepting exterior is hard to maintain for an audience of one. Distractions are hard to find. I find myself inspired in the morning, but my spirit is lagging, aimless, and I turn to the news for something by late afternoon. Aware that too much information isn't healthy, I flip through the channels until I can find something benign to watch. I could read a book. I used to love to read. It is a time like no other.

A phone call with a friend earlier this afternoon allowed me to share some of my concerns and worries, unburdening some of the woes of my anxious mind and body. As we discussed the magnitude of the impact of COVID-19, my friend was moved to pray for the needs of the world. Her expression of faith invited God's Spirit to move in people. As she prayed, tears rolled down my cheeks, my breath held tight. I murmured agreement but couldn't speak. School families everywhere are all in the early stages of grief. There's an incredible loss in all of this. Profound and deep. The world is groaning at every level. No one's life will be unmarked. This is only the beginning of mourning. Though I was and am reluctant to cry, I am also grateful. Tears are not the enemy.

March 30
11:45—lunchtime

The first day working from home. The video-chat staff meeting didn't shed any light on whether EAs will be laid off. The assumption is that we will work until the end of April.

The global COVID news is brutal. I don't think any of us can grasp what's happening in many places worldwide, including our country. To stay grounded and 'in the moment' while maintaining awareness and empathy is no easy feat. My chest hurts. And I am finally acknowledging that the shortness of breath I have is likely stress-related. I am holding my breath — a very old, ineffective coping strategy. If I am very still, I will be safe.

An explosion of emotion is building. I hear a new sense of panic in the leaders' voices as they plead for people to stay home. You can see it in every face. And never before have people been so thankful to live in Canada where, for the most part, lives matter. As I sit safely in my house, I wonder: would I be as brave as the medical professionals or other front-line workers who live in the most hard-hit places? If I had little ones at home? No one signed up for this when they became a doctor or a nurse, a grocery-store worker, a pharmacist, a truck driver, a cleaner, a factory worker, a Service Canada worker, a politician... I could go on, but once again, I have strayed from what I am feeling, what my intended purpose was. Record history. It is dreadful. Not here. Not yet...

In the United States, experts project between 100,000–200,000 may die by the end of August. To date, there are just over forty thousand cases in the United States and around 1,700 in Canada. One newscast I listened to was of an interview of a woman in her fifties who lost a brother, two sisters, and her mother. She, as well as another brother and sister, was infected but survived. I know people survive great tragedies. Nations rise. We go on. But how? It is impossible to grasp this woman's loss. Faith. Father help me. Save us. Heal our land.

March 31

The number of infected people in Alberta: 754. On March 13, the number of infected people was twenty-nine.

It is Cheri's (Mrs. Troyer) EA birthday. I sent her a well-wishing text this morning. I plan to work at the school today, so I will see her in person. Though I am looking forward to seeing everyone, there's also a sense of apprehension running through my veins.

It's the first day back to school.

I feel lost. I scan the room—no names on the children's desks. Mrs. Backlund is trying to determine who needs what. I watch. I feel like my presence is pointless with the absence of students. My brain is foggy, and I feel weak in the knees, my body slightly separated from my mind. What I am best at, that which is natural and easy, is no longer needed. I am aimless in my wandering. Not helpful at all. When our room is occupied with children, I can be cheerful, calm, and reassuring—engaged and present. Without them, I am stricken with inactivity.

The frenzy of activity in the first two weeks is now over. Still, who knows what's next? Will there be total school closures across the province? How long will EAs have jobs? Last week our jobs felt secure. Saturday's Premier Address made it sound as though the loss of our jobs is imminent. Today, it looks like we will be employed until the end of April.

Mrs. Cheri Troyer

Mrs. Troyer poked her head into our room to say, "Hi." She smiled warmly. "If you need a walk, come see me for a visit." She works with Mrs. Marshall in Grade One. Mrs. Marshall is six months pregnant and is working from home. Today Mrs. Troyer's job was putting together the children's weekly school homework packages. Mrs. Backlund needed to go to the office to sort out some work, so I made my way down the hall to catch up with my friend.

"It is just so heavy, the air. I hate this. I wish I could just blow it all away." Though earlier Mrs. Troyer mustered up a cheerful hello for my benefit, now, she is subdued. She, always the warrior, is weary and wary of what is and what may be. Her children are frightened. I am ever appreciative of her awareness and response to her children's concerns and those of the children in our school. She is sensible and caring and doesn't point fingers or give lectures. She meets people where they are at. Mrs. Troyer has a great blend of gentle encouragement and a kick-butt attitude. Her middle child just wants to feel her friends' physical bodies close to hers. Well said. Me too. It's hard to leave my friend. It's comforting to be together.

My instincts have been telling me to listen to the guidelines that say to work from home if possible. I feel a little alone. I feel like I missed valuable time with my colleagues in regard to the mission. We discussed this too. What roles do we have to play? What if the part of those who stay home matters just as much as those who cannot? It's hard on the ego, hard on connectedness. It's challenging to feel so powerless and purposeless. And yet... we agree... be wise... be safe. That is helpful, and in many cases, also selfless.

We pondered the various responsibilities of the teacher and the EA. The teachers' role is more defined. They still must plan and prepare lessons. For us, at times, our functions feel a bit elusive. Cheri commented on how drastically different the atmosphere between week one and week two was. The first week without students was almost exciting. Like a scary ride, you have to be brave on the way up, but once it starts, you hold on tight, and soon it is over. There were plenty of jobs to keep busy minds less occupied with 'what if's?' Concrete purposeful work was accomplished with a crew of like-minded others. There wasn't as much fear of risk, so social distancing wasn't practiced to the same degree as week two. Respectful, for sure, but also hard to remember. And working meant less time watching the news—the warnings. Instead, there was information shared, world news, and an odd fascination with what isn't comprehensible. If we keep doing, keep laughing, keep… keeping it away, it will bypass us, you'll see.

Back in the classroom, Mrs. Backlund is still hard at work preparing both online and paper homework assignments for the children. We haven't even had a moment or headspace for idle chat. She feels as overwhelmed as I do. My absence means Grace works alone, and she finds this very isolating. Usually, it wouldn't be such a big deal, but these are no ordinary circumstances. We don't seem to realize or admit how much we need others until they seem far away and unavailable. I thought I was coming to work today, in part, to be good support for my friend. I don't think I was.

Later that afternoon, while listening to an hour-long presentation on anxiety, I had an interesting revelation. It wasn't new, but it was a reminder and explained why I had felt hyper-aware at school. My response was involuntary. When the body feels threatened, it sends a message to the brain; a scan is done and decides whether it has experienced another memory that warns it to be on guard.

April 2, Staff Meeting

Everyone seemed a bit more chipper this morning. Their faces still showed signs of carrying heavy loads, but their voices were less wearied today. Recognizing the need for optimism and positivity, Miss Black, the Principle, queried:

1. What positive connections did you make with your students this week?
2. What is one thing you are proud of this week?
3. What is one improvement or something you would like to do this week?

The response was positive, in both spoken and written communication. It's interesting how even in the written messages in chat, people's personalities come through. One thing very apparent is how much we miss the students. Our faces lit up each time a student was brought into the conversation. This was especially so if a student responded to correspondence or a parent sent a picture of the student or their child's artwork or assignment.

Sara, (Miss Pomeroy) was highly animated as she shared how just seeing one of her little ones warmed her heart. Jessie (Ms. Kay) stayed up until midnight working with several parents and a student, solving a problem and building a crucial parent relationship. It seems as though some parents and students are getting better at communication. Emma (Miss Keddy), the kindergarten teacher, had some unique challenges with guardians and has had to figure out ways of accommodating those who have no idea how to communicate with or use new technology.

I fully empathize and am struck by how massive a learning curve this is for our staff. I was amazed at each as I listened to them share. We were now in a new world: Google classrooms; online chats; Zoom; Teams. Music lessons are a highlight for our more senior students. Mrs. V. was very wise in one of her reflections: awareness of the need to be patient and encouraging with herself and not compare her progress with others. Mrs. V. was proud of encouraging a parent with their struggling daughter. Kristina (Miss Black) commented that we have many students we are concerned for. Cheerleader that she is, she congratulated Mrs. V. on her success at engaging her students. Not just in their work, but in sharing their thoughts and enlisting them to help plan ways of continuing some classroom routines. This is a victory.

Angie's heart (Miss Craig) for children came through her voice with deep affection. She had been in contact with several families and hoped to do more. Mrs. Tollefson's (EA) sharing was in regard to an online course called Trauma-Informed Schools. Cheyenne is sensitive and thoughtful. Her words were poignant. She reminded us all of what we already know. Life is hard for some of our kiddos (many of our kiddos). We miss expressing our love for them. We miss seeing their faces, and having their little personalities make us laugh, sometimes sigh, sometimes cry.

Although the staff meeting was very positive for most, I empathize with those who are not feeling buoyed by success but rather grappling with programs and expectations—feeling alone and disconnected, like their lack of success thus far is a failure. Though I was happy for those who seemed to be excelling, as I listened to their cheerful optimism, a feeling of isolation and ineptitude tainted my attitude. In my thoughts, I am lost and alone in this new era. In times like this, I need to be mindful of being kind to myself. There is nothing easy about the trial we are experiencing.

While on a short walk, I realized one of the difficult decisions I made wasn't anything I had control over. I was sick and following the recommendations of AHS. If you are feeling unwell, stay home. Though my absence from school couldn't be helped, it still felt like I missed out on a crucial time of bonding with my school family. The daily visits were gone. I missed encouraging and refreshing one another through emotional support and physical proximity.

I also was conscious of the need to be prudent with my health. I need to stay well and COVID-free so that if my daughter or son-in-law contracts the virus, I can look after my grandchildren. My daughter works at a bank, an essential service. She has been self-isolating the last few weeks because she was in close contact with someone who had travelled. If she can find suitable childcare, she starts back at the beginning of next week. That is a troubling thought. She can't take her boys to someone she has never met before. During Alberta's lockdown, almost all daycares were closed. My worrisome thoughts are a result of a concern Grace voiced earlier today. She has two boys. What if something happens to both her and her husband? Who would take care of them? It's a practical, responsible, and disturbing question.

I found today's meeting uncomfortable because I'm not good at chatting in chat rooms. In person, I enjoy visiting with every one of our staff members. And in the last two years, I have become more open. However, when presented with new challenges, especially regarding technology, my brain freezes. I don't know why I have a block. It isn't like my brain is incapable. I fall farther and farther behind, and I simply don't try. It is a weakness. I haven't connected with any children. Again, in person, I am fully engaged. Grace and I had talked about one way I could stay connected to some of our students, which was by reading to them and listening to them read. But without permission slips, it's not possible.

April 3

Alberta's numbers are rising. The first death in the North—a young man, a friend of Ms. Kay, one of our own. There is no time for tears, no risk to hold or come undone. My heart, all our hearts, hurt for her. Week two is no longer the least bit fascinating but a grind—so much work to do. The teachers are overwhelmed by the amount of new technology they are to implement quickly. Their own families are in need. It is lonely. And big, and there are moments when it doesn't seem doable. And yet, each task gets completed on time.

Ms. Wendy Stokes

I received a wonderful gift while out walking. I knew Ms. Stokes lived in my neighbourhood, but I couldn't remember which house. Just as I was pondering which one, I heard someone calling my name. There was Wendy with a great big smile. That's one of the things I always notice. Wendy has a beaming smile and a hearty laugh. We have been allies for a long time. This is the seventh year I have sat in on her music lessons. She is a talented and knowledgeable teacher. Thanks to her, the school received a grant for several thousand dollars worth of instruments.

　　"Hold on a moment," she instructed. "I'm just going to put my coat on." A moment later, she emerged from her house. We stood across from one another, at least two metres away, and had an uplifting visit. Not that everything we discussed was positive, but it's always helpful to share your thoughts, worries, and concerns. She, like me, has a bit of a computer technology glitch or slight malfunction. Unlike me, she has no choice but to persevere through the difficulties of what is foreign to her. And in some ways, she has gained satisfaction in much of what she has had to learn. It has pushed her out of her comfort zone. Wendy is so enjoyable. It's the way she admits to struggles in a matter-of-fact manner. Wendy is direct and straightforward. She still smiles through it, with objectivity and responsiveness. Today she voiced her discomfort with not being proficient in Microsoft Teams. She described the ailments and difficulties I experienced. She also has trouble following side chats and faces popping up all over. What is a person supposed to respond to? Is there a social etiquette a person should follow?

We both acknowledged our feeling of inadequacy of not knowing what or even how to respond to this current climate. Even with teachers' best efforts, if parents and students don't engage, what is there to do? I can see how important it is for teachers and administrators to focus on what is going well. Celebrate and encourage one another. Expectations can't be what they were. And yet, I see the importance of not limiting what might be possible. It's quite a balancing act. Don't walk so close to the 'I must do better' cliff… I may trip on a stone and plunge over the edge, tumbling to the bottom, bruised and broken. Tether yourself to something or someone secure and stable.

April 6: Staff Meeting

After Miss Black presented my proposal, she allowed me to speak. Her thoughtful, supportive words had been chosen with care. Though I am rather adept at expressing thoughts via a pen or a typewriter, my speech isn't nearly as fluent. Before this morning's meeting, I finished watching Trauma-Informed Resilient Schools. Fresh in my mind, I related that people's response to trauma is unique to them. The world is in a state of trauma, and none of us will go forward unaffected by the pandemic crisis. The way forward, in every instance of trauma, is talking about the event, being supported and cared for while sharing emotions and feelings in safe environments. How we gain resiliency is through community, with supportive relationships and purpose. I feel like the process of journalling our experiences might be beneficial in our personal lives and how we relate to children in our care. We are living with uncertainty every day.

We must learn from our uncomfortable feelings and how we tend to respond to adversity. Remember the ways we express our frustration, despair, isolation, withdrawal, or denial, and how massive the challenges of online teaching felt. As well, recall the pain of having to be physically distanced from our friends and family. Remember the fear of all the 'What if?' and 'When/if'— if we can acknowledge and be gentle with our own fears and struggles, then we can genuinely empathize with others, and especially with our students and our children.

Later: so much time spent inside on the computer, learning about the brain, behaviour and trauma, I was tired and in need of a reprieve. The sun is warm and inviting; it beckons, "come walk with me." Thoughts and ideas bounce off one another. How to tie everything together? How to introduce each person? I want to capture personalities, so the reader gets a sense of the person who has invested their time and heart into their profession. One thought leads to another, and I consider the structures needed. Introduction, Table of Contents, etc. This brings a smile to my face. Mrs. Backlund would be so proud of me. Not very long ago, she taught a unit on the parts of a book. She instructed the class to choose a topic that interested them and then assemble the various components so they could make their very own book. It was an arduous struggle for some. Three little boys sat at the table in the hallway with one little Spanish girl still learning English. I was trying to encourage and prod them along. Occasionally the hallway has its own challenging activities that prove to be distracting. A disturbance momentarily took me away.

When I returned, Carly was sitting next to Anthony B, giving him ideas for his book report. "What you like? You know, movies, like… " In broken English, she named a few. It is not the first time she's stepped in to help me. She is very empathetic and sensitive to the needs of others in the room. When she notices that I am otherwise occupied by a child or circumstance, and unable to attend to the task at hand, she takes it upon herself to help me out. I laugh at this. She has scolded children, taken up a cutting job (not ideal), and enthusiastically taught Rachel how to do arithmetic! Man! I know, on some level, I have avoided writing about our classroom. People say all the time how much they love their job and the kids in the classrooms. Despite all the many difficulties, and there are many, we do. This is my seventh year as an EA, and every one of the teachers I have worked with has fully invested their time, energy, and even money into providing the very best care possible for their students.

There are many things the public doesn't see.

The absence of the children is striking. As EA, my purpose and job description are now undefined. When you can't see a child, you don't know how they are. Are they safe, hungry, cared for? Overall, our kids are pretty sweet and good to each other. To picture them can be painful. Not all the children we said goodbye to in March will return in September. We must trust that the care and instruction that we provided impacted their young lives somehow. Wherever they are, there will be another team of educators who care, and they too will be doing their best to build a strong community of support for them.

I have just one more story about Carly. Maybe two... the first day she came to school, she decided to go home at lunchtime. At the time, she spoke almost no English. I had to run after her, all the while trying not to scare her. Best as we can tell, she said the reason she left was that she wanted to play. I think, though, she was scared. Scared is not an emotion she can openly share. She has a brilliant smile; a stubborn stance; a defiant look. She's just a little girl trying to be brave. She loves school and is gentle and kind with younger, smaller children. Carly always says, "thank you."

Last story. We were in the library. Mrs. Flanagan had found us a book with four different fairy-tale stories, the current week's genre "Which one you like?" she urged me. She wanted to read to me. I picked one and asked if Carly was going to read it in English or Spanish. She twitched her nose. First Spanish. She rattled off a litany of words. She read (interpreted) with great expression. She obviously knew the story or a similar one. After she finished, she asked. "You like I read more?" "Sure," I responded. "How about this time in English?" I coaxed. "First Japanese?" she compromised. She is excellent at this skill. Hmm... "You know Japanese?" I don't really think she does. I think she is pretending; a normal thing kids do. She shows good imagination, and she is engaged in wanting to learn and share with me. She took me completely off guard when out of her mouth came, if not Japanese, a very good impression of it. Somewhere she had listened to enough Japanese to catch on to the rhythm and cadence of the language. I clapped. "Wow, Carly! You are a wonder. Where did you learn how to speak Japanese?" She didn't say but showed me with her fingers, "Japanese, just tiny bit." Opened her fingers wider. "Spanish, big." In regard to how well she speaks English, she wavered her flat hand. "Some." "Would you like to read to someone else?" I asked, sharing her excitement and wanting her to experience the same feeling of success and animation with another adult. One of our goals for Carly is to get her to be more trusting with other adults in our school. On our way back to the classroom, we met Mrs. Thomson in the hallway. Carly's eyes lit up. She wanted to read to Mrs. Thomson. She likes her and even gives her hugs sometimes. Carly is just one of many children. Truly, I could tell a cute story about each student in our classroom…

Mrs. Cathy Flanagan

Every school needs an enthusiastic and wise librarian. It is rare not to be greeted with a friendly smile by Mrs. Flanagan. She always seems willing and able to find helpful resources for teachers and students alike. She is welcoming and engaging in nature. Her duties are split between our school and another. Her lunch hour doesn't often coincide with the other staff, but she is a lively addition to any conversation when it does.

Miss Angie Craig

The first person to eagerly respond to my invitation to share was Miss Craig. Miss Craig came to Avondale's rescue at the end of September, a gift. Our school, but in particular the grade three classroom, was in need of another EA. We were very appreciative of Angie's easy nature and willingness to go wherever she was most needed. She left a school, a teacher, and a classroom full of children she loved. The beauty of Angie is that though it must have been a sad transition, she didn't seem to miss a beat. She rolled up her sleeves and began loving Avondale children and staff alike. During recess, little ones always surround her, and a hand is often being held.

Amidst the pandemic crisis, Miss Craig has remained cheerful, optimistic, and determined to foster the relationships she has developed with the children. After our staff meeting, she confided that, behind her outward appearance, her insides have frequently felt a mess. Halfway through last week, reality seemed to hit harder, and school no longer seemed safe. No place felt safe beyond her own home. Her husband, children, and pets were her comfort.

"It was so bad. Being at school or in the grocery store, my anxiety and depression really kicked in. It was so bad I was vomiting." I feel for her. And to some degree, I can relate. I, too, felt threatened at school and the few times I've been in a public place. My body is hyper-aware of danger. It is not a conscious choice. Much as we outwardly try to be okay, and tell our brain we are okay, the message doesn't get through. The body is adamant and will not be quiet. Its job is to keep us safe. It's a difficult time for the body and mind to be in harmony with one another.

"The other thing that makes me so sad is thinking about the children. The first day we had no students, I couldn't stop crying on the way home. What will happen to them? And this week, I see the fear and unease in my coworkers' faces, and I want to hug them. I am a fixer. It is so hard not to be able to hug the people you love. I just want to take away their pain." I understand. When the way you are best able to express your care for others is taken away, it's a helpless feeling. She, like me, is feeling lost. One of our jobs as EAs, especially with younger children, is providing physical comfort and safety. And Miss Craig's life mission is all about nurturing and building skills in children.

"On the positive side," she said, "I made contact by telephone with several of our students." There is a notable difference in the tone of her voice, bound in hope as she shared how good that's made her feel. The child she works closely with has yet to respond to her email invitation. But Angie is determined. She has faithfully emailed him and is resolute in her commitment to continue to try to find a way to connect with him. (Side note: I stole the word 'resolute' from the Queen's recent speech. It's only the fourth time in history she has addressed not just her Commonwealth but the entire world. She encouraged, 'Be brave and resilient. We will get through!')

Angie is worried that all the hard work and progress her little fellow has made will be lost. I assured her it wouldn't. He's had excellent instruction and loving, safe EAs over the last three years—EAs with great understanding, who were gentle but firm. Each relationship has helped build trust, making the transition from one year to the next year smoother. I don't know that to be true, but it makes me feel better to think so.

Several days later, while at school helping hand out students' work, I ran into Miss Craig. She was exuberant, face glowing, and pleased to update everyone on the progress with the students in her class. And just now, she had made physical (distancing) contact with the little boy who is her one-on-one. She was bubbling over with happiness as she described her visit. While she delivered a parcel to his family, he watched from the window. "I blew him a kiss, and he caught it! Then I threw snowballs at the window, and he put his hands together to catch them! I feel so much more settled inside now that I have seen him doing well." I commented on how happy I am that the family finally responded to her emails.

"Karen… you should have seen me. I was sitting with my family when I received confirmation, and I started to cry. I was so happy." Angie placed her hands on her chest. "My heart is full."

Mrs. Phyllis Cash (EA)

I don't know Phyllis all that well, but my experience with her is that she is friendly and intelligent. She loves to watch curling, as do I! She is sensible and practical and quietly goes about taking care of whatever needs doing. Diligent and purposeful, she is always listening for helpful programs or supplementary resources that benefit the Avondale community. She is especially fond of the little ones she worked closely with, often quizzing Miss Black for details on how they are doing. The following is, in her own words, her experience of the first few pandemic COVID-19 weeks.

Hi Karen,

Just finished taking the course, "Respect in School," so I decided to put some thoughts down. Starting Wednesday, March 11, the pandemic was hitting the news with new releases and scary information daily. My husband, Brian, had left Canada on March 5 to travel to New Plymouth, New Zealand, to be with his mom as she was in the hospital being admitted to a long-term care home. When he left, the virus was happening in China—not affecting us, so we thought.

As the news started saying all Canadian residents should return home, I contacted him. I was terrified that he would not be able to return home and be stuck in New Zealand. As he has asthma, I especially did not want him by himself in case he contracted the flu. We had booked his return flight with Air Canada. I spent four hours on hold, only to be told that it would be our choice if he came early, and we would have to book a new return ticket. When I pressed the matter, they said they would bring him home through Los Angeles or San Francisco if I wanted. This did not work as I did not want him to have to go through those airports where he could be exposed to the virus. They then said, what about flying to Sydney, Australia then through the states, but again, what if it was stuck in Australia? These suggestions were made while talking to Air Canada on three separate occasions and with various personnel. We called our insurance agent as we had purchased trip cancellation or interruption. Once the trip had commenced, we were told, meaning he had already travelled to New Zealand that they could not help.

Every time I called my husband, he did not understand the impact COVID-19 was having as New Zealand did not have any cases. On Sunday, March 15, when they cancelled all schools in Alberta, I decided he needed to come home NOW. I called Air New Zealand and booked him on a one-way ticket direct from Auckland to Vancouver. Of course, on such short notice, we had to pay over $3,400.00 as there was only one seat in Premium Economy. I then booked him on WestJet from Vancouver to Calgary and Calgary to Grande Prairie. He arrived home on March 18 just after midnight. Because he was coming from out of the country, we both self-isolated for fourteen days. Altogether, I probably spent over eight hours on different phone calls, but he was home!!

In self-isolation, we were able to watch the news together, and he understood the full impact of the virus in Canada. He received EI for three weeks and the money was just deposited in our bank this week.

The following Monday, New Zealand shut down the country and sent everyone home but emergency personnel. My husband is now back at work, and I am dividing my time between home and school.

Packing up the children's things and keeping busy was good for me as I could not watch the latest developments happening in the world. We packed in various stages, as first we thought the students would only be out for a short time. Then we were told to pack up their shoes and personal items, and finally, we were told to remove names from desks, boot rooms, etc. My biggest concern was our five PUF students from kindergarten. They need extra support and are already behind grade level. My other concern was for our students, who used to receive morning snacks and lunch from us. I was glad when I found out we would be delivering food packages to these students. My EA role was a concern for me as our teacher did not need our help with making up homeschooling packages. Kind of just came in and asked every day where I could help. Felt not very useful some days.

Phyllis

April 7

My second attempt to walk the halls of our school met with success, meaning I felt grounded. The jittery nerves of last week calmed. Today the adult me was in charge. The last two days I finally felt like myself. That doesn't mean I am unaware of the positioning of others, but I am more mindful; though my body had moments of anxiety, my mind is doing a better job acknowledging and reassuring.

Mrs. Grace Backlund

Mrs. Backlund has just gotten off the phone with a parent. Her face is pale and drawn. Another burden, not hers to carry, and yet, it is like a small punch to the stomach… one of the hazards of being a teacher. Not all updates of children are positive. She shared that she was having difficulty learning new technology, and the amount of time it takes her to type lesson plans is significantly longer than other teachers. Instead of twenty minutes, it takes her forty-five minutes. And her shoulders and back hurt. Add those challenges to her personal life, and, at times, it's all just too much. I sympathize with her and feel her distress. She is trying her best. That's what she always does. I feel helpless to ease any of her load. If only I were more willing to try. That's what the accuser says. The excuser tells me I have no valuable skills. This is what a crisis does. It attacks our character. Patience, gentleness and compassion are needed—for everyone, including ourselves. How are we to know all of the how's when we have never seen them before?

Mrs. Jae LeClerc (Vice-Principal)

While waiting for the photocopy machine, Mrs. Leclerc spotted me, smiled, and waved me over into her office. "Time to talk?" she asked. Mrs. Leclerc has a big personality, and the kids love their small-group time with her. She is the 'mother hen' type in some ways, wanting to make sure all her staff members are doing okay. She plays card games with the kids during indoor recesses and gives hugs without reservation. Sure, all circumstances can be made better with a hug. She generously offers her time for extra jobs in need of doing. Today was a difficult day for everyone because of the announcement that EA's will be laid off at the end of the month.

I think she may have felt worse than me because she was the bearer of bad news. She wished it weren't so and couldn't express enough how much she and the other teachers appreciated the EAs. It was a sad day—another loss. Oddly, the layoff news wasn't overly distressing. I knew it was coming, and though it isn't financially ideal, it is doable with government aid. I know I'm somewhat prepared to endure a little hardship. Not all people are so fortunate. My bills and needs are small, and, in a way, I see this too as a sacrifice. I'm not angry about being laid off. The province is facing catastrophic times. For me, the greater concern is the fear of loss and change.

Whatever comes, I know it won't be the same as a month ago. Mrs. Leclerc was trying hard to be okay. I could see it in her face. A lag or a pause ensued, a question or a thought unexpressed. I am getting better at addressing the unspoken. I ventured, "Would you like to participate in the process of journalling?"

Though she's been supportive and complimentary of the idea, I sensed her hesitation. Vulnerability is no picnic. And this, for her, is not the time. She didn't want to offend or discount the value, but for now, it is, "Thanks, but no thanks. Not right now. I have enough on my plate..." I assured her it's okay. We each respond differently to moments of crisis—so many factors at work. Jae is a really hard worker. Invested in every student's welfare. It's a heavy load. She is still approaching everything as business as usual, but I see the tiredness in her eyes. And, like almost all of us, careful with the movements we make with our bodies. The tiniest traces of mistrust. Like Jenga or the game with the marbles, when too many bricks or sticks get pulled out, it is only a matter of time before the whole thing comes tumbling down.

Wanting her not to feel pressured in any way, I counselled, "I don't want you to feel pushed into sharing if you're not comfortable, or ready."

I switched gears and found a topic that would hopefully put her more at ease and restore her sense of wellbeing. "Tell me about what it was like having to set up a new program. Having to adjust how you teach to empty chairs." Here, Mrs. Leclerc is on firmer ground, and her confidence strengthens. Get teachers to talk about teaching, and they become readily engaged, eager to share. She painted a vivid picture:

Leaving school on Friday to find that school was closed on Sunday was a huge shock. The unknown, the questions, the wonderings, and the rush to quickly make sense of things while trying to sort out how to deliver quality educational programming. It was like Willy Wonka in the Chocolate

Factory where the character TV, a 'rootin tooting' cowboy of a boy desperately wanted to be a character inside the television. He got his wish when he, like the other characters, ventured where they were not supposed to go. The scene explained that large pieces needed to be disassembled, allowed to shrink, then reassembled inside the television. In order to get in the actual television, he has to get into the camera and be disassembled. Then, to the horror of his parents, he flies through the sky in tiny 'bits.' The 'bits' hover above the characters who are witnesses to the disappearing boy! The scene resembled a thick swarm of Mayflies buzzing overhead before reassembling— TV's image appeared inside the actual television! The early stages of COVID closure sort of felt like that for me: a b-zillion pieces of 'bits' hovering overhead that somehow needed to be reassembled to make sense of the school closure and how we would proceed in the future.

Mrs. Cheri Troyer

Today, I put on makeup and school clothes. It helped to normalize my day.

I hadn't yet had a chance to say hello to my friend Mrs. Troyer. I wanted to see her before I delivered the two food hampers I signed up to deliver. Much to my delight, I found not only Mrs. Troyer but Mrs. Thomson as well! Now, it's hard to find two more lovely women than these, and not just outwardly, they have very beautiful souls. They looked a pretty picture, content, despite the distance of eight feet that separated them. Seeing my friends and seeing their response to me warmed my heart.

"How are you doing?" they asked. "Good, I feel much more like myself. I'm more settled inside today." From the early stages of my thought process regarding journalling from a school perspective, Mrs. Troyer has been a supportive audience and sounding board. She has already permitted me to write about anything we share regarding COVID-19, school, and all the changes and challenges we are facing.

"Just don't ask me to have to write something myself!" she laughed. No worries, it is enough to listen to her perspective. She is wise as well as discerning; honest, and kind. I trust and value her thoughts and opinions.

Mrs. Lorraine Thomson

Mrs. Thomson was comical and amusing as she used her hands and body to express how reluctant she was to partake in a one-on-one conversation. Not that she doesn't think it's a good idea. She does. Good nature and good humour allow her to poke fun at herself, admitting that opening up is no place she wants to go! Lorraine knows herself and respects where she is. She is a wonderful person and a blessing to staff and students alike.

Last Friday, before I shared my idea with our entire staff, she sent me a simple text that touched my heart. Just three words. "You doing okay?" Post COVID-19 has produced some unexpected moments of tenderness. I feel very cared for. Not that I didn't before, but now there is more transparency in our faces. It's hard to hide what's underneath. The people I work with are more than just coworkers. We see each other every day. Though we don't always have a chance to talk during the day, when we see each other, we exchange fondness, encouraging smiles, or an empathetic word or two on difficult days.

Was I okay? The Informed Trauma Resilient Schools course I watched earlier was impactful and prodded me to approach Miss Black about my idea of journalling with the rest of our staff. At times, I am apprehensive about the proposal and the honesty and quality of what I have written. In my heart, I'm convinced our bravery in accepting and embracing the process will bless us and those who read our stories. After a few moments of indecision, I answered as honestly as I could. It isn't easy to explain.

"Hi... why? That's very nice of you to ask, Lorraine. It makes my eyes mist. I've had a pretty good day. A bit of up and down. Not dark, though. Tired, anxiousness gets held in my body. How are you?"

"Just thinking about you and making sure you're okay. Why? Well, something just told me I should ask, and so I did. Yes, it's been that kind of day here, too." I smiled. I could picture Lorraine and hear her voice. She is gentle and kind. Grandmotherly. Fun. On occasion, I tease her, and she laughs with surprise. I appreciate her wisdom and approach to the children and staff alike. Lorraine has worked as an EA for over thirty years and is a wealth of knowledge. Not always with words, she is an example of how to be thoughtful and successful with children and adults.

"I'm glad you listened. The one day I was at school, I felt lost and ill at ease. Was very strange." (I felt hyper-aware, threatened, not so specifically by anyone, just my body frantically sending messages to my brain: *danger danger danger!*) "Did you read my idea that Kristina emailed everyone this afternoon?" I am wondering, is this in part the reason for her concern?

"I could tell you were jittery that day and, as you know, I don't usually act on stuff but rather keep to myself, but just thought I would check-in. Yes, I did read the idea. It's been on my mind. Don't know how to respond yet cause I'm scared of the unknown. I'll talk to you tomorrow. You take care, and if you need anything holler, and I'll try to help."

"Thank You, Father, for Lorraine. I'm grateful you put her in my life."

"You did an awesome job expressing your feelings. Maybe that's why I'm unsettled. Yes, thank you, Father, for Karen and take care of her."

April 8: Staff Meeting

Excited and pleased with her students and with herself, Ms. Kay shared that twelve of her eighteen students completed their assignments and posted them on Google Classroom!

Miss Pomeroy was eager to share. This is her first year with our school. Red hair. Vivid personality. She learns quickly and displays energetic freedom in being silly and fun, which produced an entertaining math dance video, very inventive and creative. Her students responded.

Her voice and face were less animated as she shared, "I am longing for connection…" A slight pause by everyone. Ms. Pomeroy's heart is a reflection of the entire group chat. We are longing for connection. Miss Black stepped in to cover the silence. Ever encouraging and complimentary, with a hearty, sincere and fun-loving laugh. Her kind heart is always on display. Having watched the video, she shared how hilarious Miss Pomeroy was. Miss Pomeroy bounced back. "You should have seen me talking to a bunch of empty chairs! After I asked them a question, I said, "You're right!" Her voice was bubbling in amusement. "Pretty sweet, you gotta use Loom, man. Smart Notebook too."

Brittany (Miss Hoyseth), who is covering Ms. Mergaert's medical leave is a great help to everyone by providing helpful instruction to those, almost everyone, who are having difficulties. She shared via email with Miss Black how much she enjoyed getting to meet her students through an assignment. She hooked them into responding by the lure of social media.

Mrs. V. exclaimed how grateful she is for Mrs. Thomson, Mrs. Troyer, and Miss Black as they were her hands and feet this week. She is self-isolating and relied on their help with this week's preparation for students.

To be sure, the tone was optimistic. Mrs. Leclerc summed up what seemed to be the consensus of those who shared this morning. Avondale was responding to the challenges of having their world flipped upside down.

She was reflective: "I was just thinking earlier; it has almost been one month since all of this started. If you had told me a month ago that I would be doing all the things online that I am, I would have told you; you were crazy. I didn't even know the names of some of the things I'm doing." She was proud of her accomplishment, as she should be. It takes incredible perseverance and commitment to learn new ways. I think especially so for those of us who are older. We didn't grow up with computers. Most of us probably didn't even own one until we were in our thirties. We are far behind our younger colleagues. I was both impressed and depressed.

I was impressed because I have few skills and can't imagine learning all that our staff has learned in such a short time. I could see the satisfaction and excitement in their faces. It's very fulfilling overcoming challenges. Finding creative ways of communicating and teaching is rejuvenating. I was happy for those who were feeling encouraged and motivated, believing the process is getting easier and they are seeing more successes. I was depressed because, as I listened, my brain shut down, and I couldn't hear. It is a curious occurrence how my brain responds, listening to all the different ways of communication. Click here. Go there. Download this…

Mrs. Dori Morin (Administrative Assistant)

Mrs. Morin has the enviable job of taking the parents' frustration calls. She has had to learn quickly how to troubleshoot and teach parents how to do the same. Mrs. Morin has a gift of putting others at ease and convincing them she is on their side, despite whatever the circumstances might be. She is warm and welcoming, very capable and very helpful, an even-keeled woman.

Secretaries play essential roles in schools, not just in how ordered and well run they are, but also in how cheerful they are. Cheerful, that's a good word to describe Mrs. Morin. Not just cheerful but caring. Early in the school year, I had a challenging assignment. The little boy I worked with, though sweet, had a tendency to run… I have had other children who have needed careful watching, and have had help in doing so, but this time something in my face or body language must have looked defeated.

"Oh, Mrs. Powell, I feel for you. You must need a hug." I had just spent the last hour trying to round up the little fellow from outside. Thankfully, Mrs. Quinn noticed my predicament, as she always does, and came to my aid. Even with two, it was no easy task. We were so close to our goal of securing a safe place when he slipped our grasp. Miss Black gallantry tag teamed me out. Mrs. Morin squeezed me tight. "I am always here for you if you need anything. I love giving hugs, so anytime you need one just come find me."

I was speechless and melting. I hadn't realized I looked or felt as frazzled as I did. That's Mrs. Morin.

Mrs. Grace Backlund

The next morning at school, I connected with Grace. She confessed she feels the same way I do when it comes to computer dismay. I found this interesting and a bit surprising. She is so smart.

Maybe the reason I don't excel at technology isn't about anything lacking in my brain. Grace verbalized a similar experience of feeling inept after listening to all the positive feedback during our staff meeting. It's like there is an actual blockage. Our brains shut down and can't hear or process the information coming at us. And even when someone is helping us, we sometimes have trouble spotting the icon we are supposed to press. She traced her technology injury to a rejection in grade nine or ten. I wonder… what happened to me? I had thought, in part, it's an age thing, but later I heard several parents also express their difficulties learning new computer programs.

A troubling concern that we discussed was the question *how?* Since the beginning, Grace has been saying that many of our parents are at a disadvantage because they either have limited access to the internet or don't have the skills needed to navigate new ways of learning online. It isn't enough to leave them behind because we tried and weren't able to connect or engage them.

"Technology feels cold and dismissive to those who don't get it. It feels like we are giving up on them." I agreed and queried, "So how do we connect with them if they don't respond?" This is what keeps Grace awake at night. The 'how' must be given as a solution, not presented as an unsolvable problem.

Mrs. Stacy Quinn and Mrs. Cheri Troyer

Later that afternoon, I handed out the students' schoolwork to the parents. How simple but rejuvenating. Cheri, Stacy, and I were standing outside, apart but together. A triangulated friendship of unity, care, and support. The sky was powder blue and the sun bright and warm. Cheri tilted her head to the sun, basking in its glow. "I feel the warming rays healing and soothing my soul."

The smile on Stacy's face was bright and appreciative, how she is every day, but even more so at this moment. It felt extra special, this short time we had to stand in each other's presence and share our thoughts, some worries, but mainly to encourage one another. The two are caring, sensible, and optimistic. I miss them very much. Our conversation was about this new world we live in, trying to find the positives.

"Jenna is feeling really down. We were talking, and I reminded her what they learned in Social Studies about quality of life. I asked her if we had all five things that we needed to have a good quality of life. Yes, we do; we have water, food, shelter, education and happiness…"

The other night Stacy was sitting with her family contemplating life with her husband. "How do we know what's good or bad for sure? This could be the best day of our lives. You always hear of people who look back at a day or a time and see how impactful that day was for the good." She likened the virus to a forest fire—nature's way of restoring itself. There needs to be a cleansing of the old to make room for the new. Admittedly, society has many areas that have deteriorated, values skewed or forsaken altogether. What if we needed a massive wake-up call, and this was the only way?

An important consideration for future lockdowns is the role of an EA in at-home learning. How do we help? We admitted how lost we have felt, and still feel, without students to care for. We were all under the impression EAs aren't supposed to communicate with parents concerning students. Everything is always communicated through the teacher. Very seldom are we even included in the crucial conversations concerning one-on-one students (thankfully, this is changing). Until yesterday, we thought the recent memo about strict rules and making sure contact is recorded was directed to the teachers only. Not until Miss Craig started talking about phone calls with students did we wonder.

We want to be involved and communicate with our kids. Is it okay to send cards home? There is proper vocabulary regarding what teachers are allowed to say on report cards. Does that apply here, too? Our natural inclination is to step back from our needs and expect direction from leadership. When directly working with students, we trust our instincts.

This is new to us as well. It's hard to feel good about your job when you feel like you don't have one.

I understand how missing the first two weeks has influenced my thinking. I was surprised to hear that both Cheri and Stacy felt the same way I did. They worked very hard the first few weeks. And Cheri has come to work every day and been very helpful to Stephanie.

Stacy is so thoughtful; she sent a birthday card home for Robert. Her words were careful and caring. She has great discernment, is always responsible, and never comes across as anything other than kind and sincere, yet she questioned herself. Was what she sent okay? Did it follow the rules?

April 11 – Mrs. V.

A very timely phone call from Mrs. V. came around 11:00 a.m. I had awoken, encouraged, but was quickly sliding sideways. The day before involved an emotional moment of surrendering how powerless and afraid I was feeling, acknowledging these feelings isn't effortless or automatic. Though I appreciate the value of talking and sharing with others, I am hesitant to share, and tend to deny or downplay intense feelings of loss, disappointment, rejection, or apprehension.

I try hard to be optimistic, sensible, together, and look for silver linings and blessings. But sometimes… sometimes there is nothing to do but be still, and sink into fears, doubts, and losses. Before I can let them go, I have to acknowledge they exist and that my feeling and concerns are legitimate.

I don't know where I will be in September. I know I have enough funds to last until then. But will I have a job? And if not at the school, where? My absence of marketable skills looms large. I know I have qualities that have potential, but… there is that… uncertainty.

And when will I get to hug and kiss my grandchildren again? Have a meal with my family? Walk with friends in person? Hug my coworkers when we pass by each other in the hallway? Hug my friends when I greet them hello? Share a simple touch of care and affection with another? Be steady, I tell myself. Be firm, gentle, and true. Being single isn't so bad, most of the time, but another person in my midst would help keep my spirit motivated and engaged. I didn't mean to be quite so honest. Mrs. V.'s phone call and friendship are a blessing.

For the last month or so, she has hardly had time to breathe, her mind endlessly racing. Between trying to finish completing report cards and wanting to be a supportive friend, plus managing her grief, it has been challenging. Her sole focus had been the task at hand: stay okay. Keep the vulnerable feelings at bay, so she could effectively do her job. COVID-19's menacing gaze hadn't yet fully fell upon her—that is until after Mrs. V. read my proposal and realized how much tension and apprehension the rest of the school had experienced. In response, she sent me an encouraging text. "Karen, I've read part of it, and the concept is a gift. I have been so caught up in the emotions, stress, and urgency of the past twelve days: there hasn't been time for reflection. This project will give us that. Thank you."

Mrs. V.'s story of tribulation began a few days earlier than March 11, the day WHO proclaimed a global pandemic: it began with a tragic, needless death of one of her Uganda Mission team members. Mrs. V.'s heart now ached of pain and loss, for she was helpless to ease the unbearable pain of her friends. The week ahead left little room for mourning. Report cards were due mid-week. So much to do. Compartmentalize. Mrs. V. is an extremely hard worker. She is at work by seven in the morning and often stays until seven at night. Though this is her second year at Avondale, I've only started to get to know her on a more personal level. A random meeting in a second-hand bookstore lasted an hour. We attend the same church, have friends in common, and through the course of this last year, our friendship has grown as we have been supportive of each other in small but meaningful ways— short, honest, sincere visits where and when time allows.

I knew something was wrong in her world. I could see it in her face and hear it in the tone of voice, slightly clipped and not engaging. Her movements were quicker, anxious. When I asked her about it, she admitted that she wasn't okay. But she would be. "I am exhausted and having a hard time focusing. I am going to need help from you and Lorraine during Passion Blocks." Already carrying a heavy load, the morning had brought yet another. Ms. Mergaert had stopped in for her daily five-minute morning visit. And suddenly all the worries of the past few months for her friend became actualized:

> Hearing Alison's news coloured everything about that day. I didn't feel any of the things you wrote about. Looking back, I can see why. After Alison told me she had lung cancer, I went to the workroom, holding back tears. I had to hold it together. The kids were coming in three minutes. I had to get through the day.

Mrs. V. reminisced with fondness as she shared how far back her and Alison's friendship goes. Over twenty years. They graduated together. They have enjoyed barbecues and playing games together, seen each other through divorces and deaths. Alison is the person who encouraged Mrs. V. to get back into teaching, first by volunteering in Alison's classroom, which eventually led to Mrs. V.'s hire at Avondale. Yes, she admitted, the last day of school for the kids was a blur, and COVID-19 was a distant second to the fear she felt for Alison.

Saturday, she attended a memorial for her fallen team member. Sunday, the Minister of Education's announcement that in-school classes were cancelled for the rest of the year brought total disbelief and shock. It took her completely by surprise. She had no idea that it was even a possibility. None whatsoever. Other places in Canada had recently closed their schools completely. No children or staff in the buildings for several weeks was the precaution in other provinces. Monday at school without children was a disconnect from the reality of the moment. There was a valiant attempt by administrators to provide some structure and normalcy, but truthfully, she felt like she was just going through the motions. Her head swirling, spinning, trying to grasp, what? And then, throughout the week, so much uncertainty as to what to do next. Pack up all of the kids' stuff? Only some? What about school? Everything kept changing. Not the fault of anyone. No one knew. It was unsettling.

I felt resentful that we were in school and guilty and selfish. Other people talked about the kids, worried about them, but I hadn't even caught up to everything. I was bottomed out. Thank goodness for Lorraine. We worked closely together, and so I felt less alone and supported. It was a battle in my mind and heart not to compare. I felt like I was so far behind everyone else getting packed up. Then, to my surprise, when I stopped for a second, I wasn't. At the end of the first week, Kristina told us not to do any work on the weekend. Only self-care. I listened, but it was hard. In the back of my mind, the taunt, if I don't do any work, I will be behind everyone.

The second week of post-class closure, a familiar theme rang amongst the staff: new technology. "Seems like every new program has an 'oom" sound attached to it. Brittany was generous, explaining and offering her expertise and help. Even so, there was a point where my brain couldn't take any more." Another admittance to struggling with the latest technology. I'm learning; it isn't as uncommon as I thought. It isn't just me or my tech-deficiency intelligence, but rather an actual fear of 'not getting it' fast enough and falling far behind, failing to live up to today's standards.

With her trademark steadfast beliefs, Mrs. V. turned the conversation towards that which was positive. Getting to know Cheri has been lovely. Cheri works at the end of the hall in grade one, and during a regular school day, there is little opportunity for interaction. Each day Cheri has stopped by to say hi, see how they were doing, and if they needed any help.

Having been forced into learning new ways to communicate has a few benefits. Mrs. V. will take advantage of Loom to connect with her family for Easter dinner. All of her family talking at once will be familiar and comforting.

Google Classrooms has been, if not mastered, entered into with some degree of success. Three videos of her teaching have been added to her list of accomplishments. One program is particularly challenging as you have to write everything on your smartboard backwards!

However, there are some positives she can build on. This uncertainty and learning time has provided Mrs. V. with the opportunity to connect with the students and parents who find the new programs challenging to understand and implement. She has been able to walk them through, step by step, just as she had to. First comes validating how difficult and stressful new learning can be and then encouraging the belief in the process.

The third week brought more heaviness of heart. Seemingly endless emails, and government documents, added to the mounting list of 'to do's and responsibilities. One email threatened to overwhelm Mrs. V—a two-page regarding the welfare of children. Just as educators are responsible for fostering and monitoring their students' wellbeing in a classroom setting, so too, in the virtual world. It is a stark reminder of how impactful school closures are to some of our students. And how limited we are in our ability to monitor, care, and protect students when we can't even see them, and when they don't respond to our attempts to connect.

In the first few days and weeks after the WHO declared a global pandemic, social distancing was an evolving concept. To the degree of knowledge or newsgathering done by an individual, the more comprehensive the threat COVID-19 presented. In the beginning, most people were naive, or perhaps not well informed; therefore, not overly cautious or adhering to the guidelines. In a way, this attitude helped ease some of the tensions people were feeling. They drew comfort from the physical closeness of one another. Though eerily quiet in the absence of children, at least they weren't so conscious of physical placement. All that changed in week three. Social distancing signs were everywhere. Staff members were now much more aware of their proximity to others; the underlying atmosphere was tense. Body movements once easy and natural, were now hesitant and stiff. The two-metre rule seems hard to remember and maintain, or even be possible in some instances.

Halfway through week three, Mrs. V. came down with a sore throat, forcing her to self-isolate and work from home for the required ten days. Amazingly, the timeline worked out perfectly with Spring Break. A visit planned with her son, wife, and beautiful little granddaughter was a much anticipated and needed reprieve. With each email and news update came the new way of being: social distancing, everywhere she looked, impending. Though her daughter-in-law and granddaughter were self-isolating, her son worked in the city in a high-traffic area. The latest breaking news—the discovery of asymptomatic carriers of the virus. How do we know who is safe? If we are safe? Mrs. Thomson, who works in her classroom, is in a higher risk category. So as much as Mrs. V. would love to hold her precious granddaughter, she knew the most responsible and loving thing was to stay home and self-distance as much as possible.

Mrs. Thomson has come to work every day. It's what she needs to do to maintain some sense of normal. Mrs. V. admires Mrs. Thomson's willingness and eagerness to learn new things. As well, she appreciates her generous and gracious presence in the classroom. They are good emotional support for each other, and together they brainstorm and persevere through the difficulties. Mrs. Thomson is proficient in many areas and a huge asset always, but particularly now.

"Seems in everything, right now, there is a huge learning curve. How to teach, how to love, how to care for our students and keep ourselves and others safe." Mrs. V. circled back to the beginning, the need to process and to grieve. She isn't all the way there yet. But in all of this, one thing she knows for sure, "God is still good and doing good things."

After we discussed the uncertainties of the future, we both acknowledged that though we are reasonably content with living alone, in times like these it can be lonely. There is the risk that physical isolation turns into social and emotional isolation.

Mrs. V. is very kind. She offers… "I have lots of room for another person in my house. If ever you need… "

Her invitation touches me. I know it is heartfelt, and who knows, maybe one day. At the moment, I don't fear being homeless. Jobless, perhaps; dependent on others' generosity, possibly. What I am sure of is that I am richly blessed with caring and supportive family and friends. Despite what I see or feel, I trust God will always make a way.

As Mrs. V.'s students headed into break, she gave them an inspiring assignment: kid-friendly information on COVID-19, ways they could do their part, stay safe, and remain mentally healthy. Three weeks of journalling and day planning. What could they do each day to make someone else's day better? I love the idea! Routine plans and being focused on others, a noble goal.

April 16 – Miss Sara Pomeroy

If you look in the dictionary next to the word 'extrovert,' you will find a picture of Miss Pomeroy: talkative, sociable, lively, optimistic, twitchy, active, assertive—an outgoing, expressive person.

We had a lovely visit this morning on Teams. Sara told me she purposely booked our meeting early so she wouldn't have to wake up alone. She yawned. Sleep has been elusive these past three weeks. Once a good sleeper, the absence of a sound, restorative sleep now takes a toll on her physical energy. She is desperately missing connection. She has been mindful of the importance of mental health and seeking out friends and family virtually. When I asked Sara what stood out as the most impactful event of the first-month post students, her response was immediate.

"I didn't know." She hadn't been following the news. She felt utterly blindsided by the events that were to come. She had booked a personal day on March 13, hoping to take a breath of air from the overwhelming week. So much pressure to finish report cards. Sara acknowledged that her anxiety levels that week were higher than usual. People don't always associate extroverts with anxiety. In her sub plans was a cute art/language project for the children, cardboard frogs they could read to. She was looking forward to Monday, to seeing how their crafts turned out. Little kids' art projects always seem to reflect their personalities. We, the adults, enjoy looking at them displayed in the hallway.

"It hit me really hard! I didn't even get to say a proper goodbye to my kids! It was a huge shock. Even going to school on Monday, it didn't register that the kids weren't coming back. A group of us even went out for lunch. We look back now and think, what were we thinking! I was slow packing up the kids' things. I didn't want to do too much; they might be back in a few weeks once it was safe and things were back to normal." Across the hall, the contrast in rooms is stark; Mrs. Marshall's room is stripped clean (by two doers, Steph and Cheri!).

"It was towards the end of the week when I first really got scared and realized whoa... this is real. The grocery store shelves were bare, something I had never seen before."

The second week Sara found herself sick with a cough and slight fever. Did she have coronavirus? She had all the symptoms. Regular temperature checks. Online assessment. Could be. Not likely... but what if?

"Man, I just miss them (the kids) so much. I feel like I lost eighteen of my closest friends. No matter what was happening in my personal life, I had them for six and a half hours a day. It already felt like my mental health was fragile... "

She paused for a second. I think perhaps it wasn't exactly the emotion she was trying to express. Fragile implies easily broken, or sometimes, in my past interpretation, shattered or weak. I now prefer to view 'fragile' as a cautionary measure, used to instruct and describe that which is precious, requiring careful tending, as not to injure. Like our hearts and minds.

"They're my children. My one stable, constant I could always count on. I hated the weekends and looked forward to Mondays. School is my safe place, my support system that I rely on."

Sara's care and connection to the children are evident in every word and body movement. Her once slightly sleepy gaze, now awake and engaged as she talks about her kids' successes: "Blows my mind what we've learned."

How did she manage the stress of teaching from afar? She took a wise and mature approach. "I lowered my expectations for both myself and the parents and their children. I took a laid-back approach. How are you supposed to be great at something you've never done before?" She is proud of her accomplishments. It's no small feat what teachers across the province and country have had to adjust to.

She started small and asked some pertinent questions. In some respects, her students' parents were now her substitute teachers. Her job was to educate the parents with new programs and give them simple instructions built on fundamentals: pen and paper, structure, and routine, while being mindful to use non-teacher vocabulary. The other part of her job was to do what she does best: be goofy and silly, expressive in a way that made the children giggle as they learned.

The mother of one of her students was instrumental in helping Sara test and set up Google Classroom. One test video she made was of herself dancing to a song that she regularly played for the class. She recorded herself singing the song and sent it to the little girl with the helpful mother. At the end of the song, she cheered, "Good job reading, your teacher is proud of you!" Anna (the student) responded with a picture of herself, "I love Miss Pomeroy." The importance of engaging the parents to send photos of schoolwork isn't just for morale but also for assessing work and keeping accountability. What Miss Pomeroy wants most for her students is that they enjoy learning, feel empowered, and challenge themselves to do their best without expecting perfection. For each child to feel happy, safe, and secure.

In wrapping up, she applauds the wisdom and nobility of taking on this project.

"History only happens once, it's our job to take it seriously."

April 16 – Mrs. Stacy Quinn

Mrs. Quinn is one of the most sincere and earnest people I have ever met. She is hard-working, conscientious, and thoughtful. Stacy is always, it seems, two steps ahead, whether in the classroom or life in general. Yet, she is humble and kind and never makes others feel like they are two steps behind. She has a lovely smile and often a slight chuckle of pleasure and amusement in her demeanour. Overall, in describing her, I would say she radiates a sense of well-being: content, calm, and capable.

Late January is when most of us became aware that China was experiencing a severe influenza outbreak that may have consequences for the rest of the world. We couldn't begin to comprehend what was to come. For Stacy, this news triggered the realization that her family may have to cancel the trip they had been planning to Vancouver Island since last summer. The thought was hugely disappointing. With well-reasoned logic, cancelling their trip seemed the most prudent thing to do. Life continued as usual. Between school and kids' activities, life was full, and life was good.

A month later, when schools in Washington State closed, a shadow of apprehension was cast upon her brow. All the world's eyebrows were raised when the NBA indefinitely paused their league, and a day later, the NHL followed suit. Event after event cancelled. Our eyes widened, alarmed but not shaken. It all happened so fast. Each day brought enormous changes around the world, but it hadn't yet touched our community.

The week before school closures, health concerns for herself and her father-in-law added to the quiet chaos that kept mounting. March 11, Stacy received a phone call from her children's swimming teacher. All lessons were postponed. Not only that, East Link Recreation Centre was shutting its doors. "That phone call made me sit back and say, 'Whoa, this is serious.' Right afterwards, minor league hockey was also cancelled. You know how much people here love their hockey. I really started to feel like, oh oh…"

"Even though there had been talk in the staffroom of stocking up for two weeks of emergency supplies, I was one of those people who didn't listen. When we got the email saying there was a meeting after school, it made me nervous all day. What were they going to tell us? Were we all being sent home and not coming back? I could sense the fear and panic in everyone. The not knowing.

Another thing that really stands out for me is Robert. He was off all day." Stacy worked one-on-one with Robert in Grade Two. This year she spends time with him in the last block of the day. She knows him well. He has come a long way through the consistent, arduous efforts of relationship-building between them. He has other positive adult relationships within the school, but this one, I think, is the most impactful. As Stacy recounted her memory of him, her face saddened. "I could tell he was having a rough day. He couldn't seem to focus on anything, and I wanted him to have a successful day. That last hour we sat in the hallway playing Jenga. It was weird. He knew enough to be worried. He said of East Link closing, 'There goes my birthday.' He was right. His birthday was a few days ago."

"I went to get groceries that weekend and couldn't believe my eyes!" Her eyes got bigger as she shared the experience, a potent reminder of the times we are living in. "The shelves were bare! I took pictures. There was no milk to be had—not whole milk, two percent, skim, not even almond milk, and then seeing the gas prices plummet…" This all added to the anxiousness of preparing for something you can't wrap your head around. The undercurrent of fear is always present. We are okay. Our lives are different. But we are okay. We will stay okay. Those we love will remain okay.

Stacy, too, was shocked on Sunday as she listened to the Minister of Education announce school closures. The sudden decision was stressful for parents whose children needed to be cared for. What was she supposed to do for childcare? Her husband had to work, and grandparents weren't supposed to be physically close to their grandkids. The initial belief was that although kids were likely immune to becoming ill with the virus, they were potentially super-carriers, placing the elderly vulnerable population at risk if exposed to them. Not given much choice, she opted for the only thing she could do, ask her parents to watch her children for the first few days.

At school, the uncertainty continued. Each day, a change in the plans. The presumption from listening to the news was that in-school learning was cancelled for the rest of the year. Every child would advance to the next grade in September. Yet our local School Board was uncertain about what children's possessions to send home. The contents of school bags to be sent home kept changing. "We packed up their things three times! First just pencils and paper, then their personal items, then everything. It was stressful. Same as for our jobs. First, our jobs are secure, then they are being cut immediately. Then not yet, but maybe."

Again, I see the tension on her face and hear the anxiousness of the moment. Sharing is reliving. Alberta Health Services was urging everyone who did not have to be at work to stay home. After the bulk of cleaning out classrooms was finished, staff members were permitted to work from home. "I felt like I was hearing two messages and was torn. One, go to work and keep your job, or listen to the guidelines, stay home with your family, and risk losing your job long term. It was such a dilemma. All your life you hear work hard, show up to everything, or your job might be in jeopardy. This was just the opposite. Who do I listen to? Then Justin Trudeau came on the air and said, "This is not the time to worry about your job. Stay home. Work from home as much as possible." She chose to listen to Canadian and Alberta Health guidelines. Stay home as much as possible and go to school on the days when extra help is needed.

"This is the first time my husband and I have ever been scared financially. We have always had jobs, always known we could find another or had a plan in place to leave one job for another. With both of us being laid off, it's scary. We live paycheck to paycheck and can't afford a delay in an EI payment." What I know of Stacy is that she is very wise. She makes good choices for her family's present and future. She appreciates the value of sacrifice, balancing needs and wants, investing in the future, and, therefore, she's very careful and responsible with how she spends and invests her money.

"We are worried about the value of our house. Everything we have worked so hard for over the last twelve years we could lose. We could lose our security blanket." My heart goes out to her. They have done everything right. Today is maybe the most vulnerable I have ever witnessed Stacy. Her fears and pain were validated, a truth for so many people around the world. She is also a pragmatic and determined woman who knows how to persevere through painful and challenging times. She will adapt.

"Everything is different in the way we have to plan. Grocery shopping, often the item you want isn't available. I used to shop once a week for what we needed that week. Now, when I see something I know we will need, I have to buy it when I can."

"Is this something you want to share?" I asked in regard to feeling the financial crunch. "Yes, for sure." Stacy has been very supportive of my project. A good sounding board. I miss my school family.

April 17 – Mrs. Cheri Troyer

Simply typing my friend's name brings a smile to my face. Of the people I work with, I have known Cheri longest. I remember the day she walked into our kindergarten classroom, a welcome angel. Eight Puff children (coded speech/behaviour/special needs) and only one-and-a-half EAs to start the school year. I had just one year of experience, and Cheri was brand new to the Puff world. It was a busy and interesting group of little people! We quickly stepped into rhythm with one another, often anticipating a need before it was spoken. There are many things I admire and appreciate about Mrs. Troyer. What is foremost in my mind is how gentle and loving she is with all children, not just the children in her care. She seeks first to nurture, then to understand. She is insightful and wise. I have been the beneficiary of her loving, kind heart many times. She is also a powerhouse that seldom runs low on fuel. Even in the most difficult days and circumstances, she chooses to look forward, not focusing on the problem but on the solution.

We haven't worked in the same classroom for five years now, but still, our eyes light up when we see each other in the hallway. Often a hug. Check in. How are you? I appreciate that this type of greeting between staff members is likely a rarity in most school settings. And it makes me sad to think it may be no more. I find these interactions helpful for our students, especially some of our one-on-ones to see the sincere love and affection we have for one another. Not that all the staff members are huggers or need to be. Some people are less comfortable, or maybe less in need, or it's just not who they are.

Being physically demonstrative with anyone other than my children wasn't part of my makeup. I didn't grow up in an overly affectionate home. It's a testament to growth; how natural it now seems to greet my friends in this manner. When I became a mother, my need to nurture enabled me to express love through gentle hands and words.

Mrs. Tollefson is another coworker who likes to greet me in the hallway with a beautiful smile and heartwarming embrace. Sometimes Sandy (Mrs. Bailey) (EA) and I simply hug with no words. We don't have to speak. It's mutually understood—I see you today. Be well; take care. Both Miss Black and Mrs. Leclerc have open arms that they willingly offer to both students and staff alike. Miss Pomeroy will never say no to a hug. And the children readily throw their arms around teachers, especially Mrs. Thomson and Miss Craig.

Meeting with my coworkers isn't just about gathering information to record history. It is more about connection, understanding, and empathy. My hope and desire are to transfer their experiences and heartfelt sharing onto paper in a way that honours them.

April 18

I am restless today, tired. Time is a funny thing. It's funny how we relate to it and how our perception of it changes, how we manage, measure, and value it. Yet, in so many ways, it is elusive… Time is ambivalent to our plans, regrets, fears, expectations, and uncertainties. It is neither kind nor threatening. It simply is. Like us; we simply are. The only ticking of the clock that is truly relevant and impactful to our beings is the now. Moment to moment we live, our actions and experiences of yesteryear are carried forward from the past, and our actions of today create how we appreciate time in our tomorrows.

Cheri and I have had a few chances to visit, but this is the first time we sit across from one another. Though it is a virtual visit, it is still comforting for me to share the last few days of difficulty, sadness, and pain. Despite the pain and tragedy of my friend's son's death, and the news of how much my mother is failing, I was reasonably peaceful.

Cheri has a friend who works at the care home where my mother lives. She knows my mom and has gotten a kick out of some of my mom's stories and antics. This makes me smile, and my heart feels a little better knowing she has caring people. She won't be alone. Visiting a dying loved one in care homes isn't a given during the COVID crisis. I am very torn. Tomorrow is April 19, the tenth anniversary of when my sister died from cancer. My mother was with my sister. There's a small trickle of worry. Even though my mom has dementia, is seldom able to follow conversations, and can recognize her family members less and less, I wonder—does her mother's heart remember?

Mrs. Troyer

Back to Cheri and our visit. She's had a very relaxing Spring Break, surprisingly so. For her, going to work each day brought some sense of normalcy. With Mrs. Marshall sensibly cautious and working from home, Cheri's days are structured and purposeful. The daily routine of assembling the children's weekly work brings comfort by its normalcy and sameness, cutting and gluing with care, photocopying. Simple but extraordinarily helpful for both she and Mrs. Marshall. Seeing other staff members each day is also refreshing.

"I was not looking forward to being at home all week with nothing to do, but it's been really good. Lots of walking and hikes. Time with the kids. Kimberly has come up with theme night suppers! Sundae Monday, Taco Tuesday… " Cheri's face was freer of care today. "It has been nice to putter and be outside. Each day I've made plans for me and for the girls. Then we have a nice family supper and evening is time to relax. I don't think I realized how much I needed this."

It's amazing how we learn how to cope, to put aside feelings and facts that impede our ability to function at our best. It may seem effortless, but it isn't. It takes tremendous effort to always be calm and competent in extremely stressful circumstances and uncertainties. Even for those who excel, as Cheri does. Skilled at sensibility, she sees that the only way through something is to admit that it is in the way. If the obstacle can't be removed, then one has to learn how to adapt.

"This (COVID-19) is our new normal. We can't change that, so instead of being mopey and looking at it as a problem, we have to look for solutions. What can we do? Everyone is in the same position. The pace is slower. And time is not such a big deal." Always such a positive perspective. Her voice was cheerful. Our conversation was encouraging. We spoke at the same time, stopped, and waited for one another. We laughed at ourselves when we both spoke again at the same time. Another thing Cheri is doing to keep her brain and body healthy is learning a new workout. She thrives on new challenges, especially through exercise. Recently, though, her sleep has been disturbed. Her husband took a huge pay cut but thankfully wasn't laid off. Still, it is stressful, and she found herself awake in the middle of the night calculating.

"I think," okay, if we move this money from here to there and we can cut back here and here…" She moved her hands. Her face was thoughtful as she shared and mimed her thought process and the worries that keep her awake at night. Then she laughed and said, "I tell my brain, "This is not a nighttime job, it is a daytime job!" We both laughed with affection at our silly but lovely, precious brains.

April 20 — Staff Meeting

An update on Mrs. Marshall's 'baby bump' started the morning off in a cheerful manner. Miss Pomeroy and Mrs. Morin showed off their new haircuts. Perhaps both will have new side jobs next fall. Miss Black encouraged everyone to keep at what they are doing. Don't compare with where others are at, instead pick out something each of us can do a little different. Have expectations, but make sure they are realistic. It's not easy. Were there any other successes besides the bravery of cutting one's hair? Mr. B (Buziak) and Miss Stokes made a little boy in their Grade Two class very happy with a surprise Zoom birthday wish. Miss Black and Mrs. Leclerc also got to participate and witness how impactful the moment was.

Mrs. LeClerc is good at stepping in when, for whatever reason, the staff is quiet. First, she updated us on how Alison was doing. "Doing okay. Hanging in there." Jae had been very busy sewing masks. Her motivation: her daughter recently graduated from nursing school. Mrs. LeClerc is an expert seamstress, and the design and quality of her daughter's masks are envied and admired by her coworkers. This prompted a short discussion on the use of masks everywhere. Miss Pomeroy was goofy as she showed off two masks. Mrs. Marshall, the Grade One teacher, doesn't have a mask yet and was reprimanded by an elderly woman while at the grocery store because she was pregnant and not protected. Mrs. LeClerc and Miss Black were quick to assure Mrs. Marshall that they would find her a mask. Who could have ever guessed wearing masks in public places would be an expectation or possible requirement?

Mrs. LeClerc gave a shout-out to Mrs. Quinn's son Logan, who is in her Grade Two class. He was very enthusiastic about participating in his latest science assignment, and his mom, Mrs. Quinn, posted some of his work and words of excitement online. She smiled fondly at the mention of her son's name, "He loves it, he takes his thermometer everywhere! Yesterday he had it out in the snow!" This made Jae happy. We all, it seems, are just a little more sensitive and tender. A little more… everything. Softer. Missing and grateful to hear each other's stories.

"He is the wind beneath my wings," Jae quipped with affection and what seemed like a tiny trace of vulnerability.

April 21 — Miss Emma Keddy

Miss Keddy is our Kindergarten teacher. She has a radiant smile that conveys warmth and welcome, the perfect disposition for working with little ones and adults alike. I don't know her well, but I sense behind her soft brown eyes there is a bit of mischief and fun, an easygoing, kind and gentle heart. She is seemingly content within herself. Still, talking to someone you don't know very well with the knowledge that your thoughts and feelings will be on display for all the world to see is intimidating. I get it. I do. At times I wonder about what I've written regarding my thoughts and feelings… my soul laid bare… it is a scary thought. Past wounds and reactions, scars each of us bears, make us leery of doing such a foolish thing. To willingly allow our hearts to be open and unprotected. And yet, the truth is, that this is when beautiful tenderness, love, care, and acceptance flourishes.

7:45 a.m. An early morning text from Emma gave me more clues into her character. "Hi, Karen! I think I have changed my mind about the journalling project. I'm going to back out. I just don't feel like I would have good answers for you. Haha. Sorry about that." She is conscientious, thoughtful of my time by texting me early.

"Good morning, Emma! It is not about having good answers! Why don't you have a visit with me? You don't have to share anything deep if you don't want to. I can write what we talk about, send it to you, and you can see what you think. You can even share a cute story if you want."

"Ok, I'll give it a try." She is a little cautious, but it doesn't take much coaxing to get her involved in something unfamiliar. She is placing trust in me, as is everyone who works at our school and shares. It is a privilege to get to tell their stories. It is also a tiny bit nerve-wracking. Did I capture their thoughts and feelings correctly? Have I accurately portrayed them as was my hope? Did I get the facts right? How will they feel?

First-year teachers are bound to have some challenges as they navigate and develop their classrooms and teaching style. The kindergarten world is unique. Though it has many structures and daily routines, it is unpredictable. It's very much a hands-on approach. Learning through play and social interaction is equally important to knowing letters and their sounds and how to count. EA support is always needed and appreciated, but for young teachers to walk into a room with three seasoned, mature (like me, older) professionals, it can be slightly intimidating. Those were some of the challenges Emma successfully addressed and worked through the first half of her rookie year. It takes time for a classroom to take shape and find its rhythm. The kindergarten classroom is in a separate wing, and Emma only works in the morning. This has made it hard for her to get to know the rest of the staff. She misses out on the small things, such as visits at lunchtime, working in the same hallway with the rest of the school, assemblies, and outdoor recesses. All are opportunities for the rest of us to connect, bond, and work in unity with one another.

Emma, like most people, had been following the COVID news. She wasn't fretting but was trying to think ahead, aware that schools in Alberta may close for a few weeks around Easter.

"Everything happened so fast! I had no idea schools would be closed so soon! It blew my mind that Friday was the last time I was going to see my kids. And things kept coming and changing. That first Monday back was so strange. It was eerie... putting all their stuff in bags." She was describing what other teachers and EAs had shared with me. Recounting this moment, a month later, I can still hear in her voice just how desolate it must have been. Stillness. Emma searched for a word or was perhaps unsure about sharing the word best suited.

"Morbid. It was morbid. They were all gone. They just disappeared. Here one moment and gone the next." I remember packing up some of my sister's belongings when she passed away. Again, I see how each of us deals with loss in our own way. Some are quick, task-oriented, don't think, and just do. It will hurt less. Others try to hang on to things or stop and reflect. Memories. Fondness. It's hard to focus, especially when everything keeps changing. Thankfully, our school children aren't separated from us by death, but to be sure, it is a loss for both them and us. The word Emma found fits.

She was also laid off from two of her three jobs, a significant loss in income. And the way government aid plans are structured, she is yet to be included in any aid packages. The second week was a pressure cooker. Again, I can hear it in her voice. Her words flow faster.

"I felt like I had to get going. I had to be quick—so many expectations. I felt like I was behind. Kindergarten chatrooms where everyone was posting all these great ideas and things they were doing made me anxious. I realized I had to shut it all out. I decided I needed to keep everything as simple as possible, otherwise, it was overwhelming, and I felt like I was being a bad teacher. I knew it wasn't fair to judge or compare my classroom to others." It takes a certain amount of awareness and self-confidence to see this: wisdom and maturity.

"I really don't like distance learning, but I do see how some kids are benefiting from the one-on-one instruction. Unfortunately, those are the same kids who were already doing well. It takes a bit more planning."

"The third week, I felt anxious too, but it was more the expectations I was putting on myself. And then we were told we were supposed to go to paperless teaching. How? It's kindergarten and not how I teach. I got into power mode and got ahead of the game. I printed three weeks' worth of work, so since then, it's been pretty chill. The videos I've made have been of me reading the kids a story. I hope they get to see it." Pause. "I don't know that they do. And I worry. How are they being taken care of? Did they have lunch today?"

I asked Emma, "What's been helpful for you?"

"Getting back to trusting myself. Not overcomplicate things. I could use so many different platforms, but I have to teach the way I teach. Learning to be okay with doing the best I can. I have supportive people I talk to and lean on."

"The hardest part is that they took the fun part of teaching away. I had all these fun and intricate crafts for the kids to make; now I had to make everything simpler."

I feel for her. Little kid crafts are the best. We, the staff, get joy helping and watching them put their hearts into projects.

"Nothing is the same." What I am hearing is ache, loss...

April 22 – Miss Brittany Hoyseth

"Team player, definitely," Ms. Kay replied in response to my request for descriptive words. I nodded in agreement. The afternoon had barely begun, and already I had witnessed Miss Hoyseth walk several teachers through complicated computer problems. I also asked Mrs. V. to share her observations and interactions with Brittany. "She is a gift. Patient, generous, helpful, willing and available, outgoing and friendly, and positive." Having played competitive sports, I easily connect to and appreciate the character traits needed to be a good team player, the very attributes Mrs. V. had listed regarding Brittany.

Adaptability is another of her strengths. Playing and coaching sports has helped her be more confident walking into new places or situations. As well, being bounced around the district for the last eight years has toughened her. She has taught Grade 1, 2, 5, 7, and PE Grades 1–8. Even so, she found it comforting to walk into the school and be greeted by the familiar faces of Miss Black and Mrs. V. EAs Miss Craig and Mrs. Bailey were additional welcomed surprises. And Brittany's openness to pop into classrooms or meetings to say hello and offer assistance in areas where she is skilled has made her feel useful and welcomed.

Seeing her transition into virtual learning and a strange home, one would never guess where her overall state of mind was. "Scatterbrained, that's the biggest feeling I remember from my first week of work. I have worked in the system for eight years. I was always covering positions. It's not been easy. I feel like I've been tossed around the last two years. In January of this year, I was hired for a part-time position for Grade Six pull-outs and PE Even though it was only part-time I felt at home and was happy there. I got a call on March 19, asking if I would be willing to transfer to Avondale for the remainder of this year as a full-time Grade Six teacher. I was given only hours to decide." Her eyes are bright, as is her smile. It is amusing, now… But can you imagine having to decide so quickly? What an unnerving scenario, walking into a classroom full of desks, once inhabited by noisy, unruly curious, eager little minds to mold, now void of any remembrance of them. The anticipation of meeting in person vanquished.

"Besides Grade Six being a grade I haven't taught, the biggest challenge I face is that I am all about relationship building. How do I do that when I have never met my students? And some I won't? It is all so strange." I pressed her further. "How so?" I was after what she was feeling on the inside. When the skills and natural gifts you count on seem as though they are taken away, what then?

Brittany tipped her head slightly, thinking, remembering. "A disconnect is what it felt like. I am all about relationship building. At first, I only had a list of names, then some pictures to go with the names. I have gotten to know the kids better. I am a techie so that part of the job has been good. I went right into Google Classroom. I sent them a video introduction of myself and my dog."

She showed me a picture of her cute little dog named Rocky, attired in a Toronto Blue Jays dog jersey. "Just over half of them sent a video back of themselves. It was interesting to see how diverse the class is. There are kids from all over the world. I got a glimpse into some of their personalities."

She shared some of the unexpected ways she has been able to interact with the kids. She noticed that many of them were engaging on the message chats in Google Classroom stream to ask her questions and were getting pretty comfortable. So much so, that she caught three of her girls engaging in negative behaviour towards another classmate. Brittany stepped in immediately to stop it from continuing and was rewarded with three, "Sorry, Miss Hoyseth." A real teacher/student moment. "I like to be organized, and I am a planner and have been working with Google Classroom right from the get-go, so moving to paperless teaching has been pretty painless for me."

"What do you like best about being a teacher?" I queried, aware that until today we were strangers, and though she appeared comfortable, an easy question would likely be welcomed. The good-natured smile that had graced her face for our entire conversation stretched wider, voice surer. "Getting to know the kids for sure and differentiating how they learn best. Engaging them. Not all kids learn the same, I want to be able to reach every kid."

As to COVID, she hasn't been too concerned, not since her parents returned home from Panama. That was a little stressful. Mostly because she missed them, her family is close-knit and used to spending time together. Brittany's parents were quarantined for two weeks upon returning home, making it a month before she could see them. As she described her and her sisters' preparation for their parents' return into isolation, she looked pleased—reflecting affection and pleasure that they could help practically. The coronavirus hasn't affected her day-to-day life. She's comfortable being at home by herself. Though somewhat extroverted outside her home, once tucked in, she is content.

"Thank you for sharing, Brittany, I know it was kind of an odd first acquaintance."

"I liked the idea of what you are doing, but I thought, 'I don't know if that's for me!' Talking with you was nice, thanks for stopping in and asking me in person. Sometimes I just need a little push to join in."

Admittedly, few people have been enthusiastic about sharing their feelings. Though the idea of journalling our experiences isn't discounted as having merit, people, including myself, are cautious of dredging up, going deeper, and exposing our most tender parts. On the one hand, it's the perfect time to be vulnerable. We are all experiencing some degree of fear and uncertainty. Our emotions and thoughts aren't so different from one another. We aren't alone. This reminds me of something Mrs. Thomson said this morning. I hope she doesn't mind me sharing. "Why did I spend and waste so many years... ?" She didn't need to finish. I understood, and everything about her said so much, so perfectly. It was insightful and wise.

Mr. Ray Buziak

I had yet to touch base with Mr. B., so I popped into his classroom for a visit. He is interesting to talk to, with often a trace of humour in his words or facial expression. He used to tease me about how bundled up I was at recess time. But I see this year he wore his toque and mittens more often! He is the only male teacher and the elder of our staff members, quiet-mannered but not shy. I have never worked in his classroom, but he is soft-spoken and kind. He is steady and predictable, making the environment a safe place. He likes to joke with the kids. When his humour slips over their heads, his adult audiences, EAs, Mrs. Tollefson and Miss Craig, are amused and appreciative. Today we sat down for an 'off the record' visit. He is intrigued by my shared journalling project. But does he want to share? In mock pretence, he turned his body as if to shield something precious or secret he didn't want to be uncovered.

"I am holding aces, and I don't want you to know." It was funny. Angie and I both laughed. Funny, but a truth acknowledged. He is a bit of a philosopher, well read, and his musings are introspective. He turned the tables, and I found myself sharing why I was doing this. What made me think of it? And to what end? He appreciated my answers and wanted to contribute his thoughts and experiences through his own writing. That would be awesome. I can't begin to tell someone's story as thoroughly as I would like. Age has wizened us, made us pause, sometimes less impulsive, more aware of the long-lasting consequences of our actions. Does he want to be vulnerable, share his truths on paper where they can never be retracted? Yet, his wealth of experience also allows him to process for himself and maybe help others.

"Just start writing, include every thought you have, then you can go back and edit. Decide what you are willing to share." A few weeks later, I received the following in my inbox.

Hi Karen,

How are you doing today? That's an interesting idea you had. I'm not sure if this fits into your plan very well or not.

Gosh, it's hard to believe it's been six weeks of all this. You were asking about our reactions and how we felt about all this. My first thought was about the big hole this puts in kid's education and how much of a concern that will be in the long run. Years ago, I read about a school system somewhere in the world (I don't remember where, Scandinavia, maybe?) where kids actually don't start going to school until ten years old. That's probably an outdated concept now, I suppose because the world changes so fast and so much. At the time of the second report card, I had two students with extensive absences in my class. One had missed fifty days and the other, forty days. Now you can tack on more time. Yes, they are getting material sent home so learning can continue, but these two students are not doing the work that's sent to them. So, instead of getting ten months of grade two, they probably get about three months—a third of normal. These two were already lacking the skills they should have had at this stage of their education. So where will they be in fifteen or twenty years in a technologically advanced world? I don't know what will become of them.

For me personally, it's definitely a change in routine. My thoughts turn to family almost immediately. I go to Edmonton several times a year and always stop in to see my oldest son. Those visits have been put on hold, of course. I suppose I could still go there, but I doubt if any hotels are open. Lots of them around here are closed so that must be true there, too. I worry about him, too. He lives alone and has had some anxiety issues in the past. I think he's only left his condo a couple of times since this all started. He keeps busy at home and does some exercising in the condo, but that much time cooped up is not good for a person's mental health.

I have a daughter in Calgary, so the same is true there in terms of visits. She's been getting out and going for walks and taking online courses, so that's a help. We talk often, too, so I can kind of keep track of how she's holding up. She seems to be okay so far—fingers crossed.

My youngest sister has two school-aged boys. She just left her husband recently, so they are all adjusting to their new life.

Throwing COVID into the mix makes it that much tougher for them. I talked to her recently. It seemed like she had her feet under her, although the finances are very tight. She is able to work from home, so that's a good thing that will help keep her going, but having to do homework with her boys adds another layer of stress, I'm sure.

And then there's my mother. It's her 90th birthday this summer, and I was looking forward to her birthday party. Now it seems like it will pass without much fanfare. It's not that we can do an online celebration of any sort. She has no computer or tablet. She has a cell phone which lays buried deep in her purse. More importantly, I shudder to think what would happen if she contracted COVID. I'm not sure she would make it—not a good thought. My mom's not necessarily a rule follower either. She goes to visit other people in her condo building and goes across the street to the stores all the time. I have no idea what precautions, if any, she takes. She lives alone and won't carry her Lifeline with her, so she could be sick (or worse) for a while before anyone knew about it. She had a fall a few months ago and hit her face on the bathroom counter on the way to the floor. I have no idea if she passed out and then hit her head or if she fell, hit her head, and knocked herself out. Anyway, that's not a good thing. We have no idea what caused the fall and neither does she.

My youngest son lives in the Grand Prairie area with his wife and daughter. I see them every week, but I wouldn't want to see that little five-year-old get sick. That would be hard to deal with, for sure. They're pretty careful, so that's good to know.

Well, that's the scoop on this end. Take care and have a good week!

Ray

Mrs. Cheyenne Tollefson

Cheyenne… (the youngest on our staff by a decade). There is perhaps none more lovable than her. Our whole school fell instantaneously in love with her upon her arrival, just over a year ago. In some ways, she is laid back and easygoing. Either a massive smile graces her face or an introspective gaze. She has an insightful mind and a caring heart. Occasionally she has a stern voice but only when absolutely necessary. Truly she is a beautiful soul that lights up every space she is in. She is also somewhat shy and reserved and chose not to share her thoughts. I asked if she minded if I occasionally mention her name and say how much I miss seeing her in the hallway and saying hello with a hug. Sometimes these are group hugs when our one-on-one students join in, adding to the cheerful, well-wishing spirit of joy or infusing energy or peace for the day.

April 23

Three people were in the staffroom today at lunchtime, all appropriately spaced apart. Mrs. Troyer was the first lovely face to welcome me. Her smile got bigger as she gave me the extra space required to maintain my comfort of two metres. Once sitting across from her, I was at ease.

An observation: though the staff is doing their best to be mindful of social distancing, I think few are worried or concerned about having another in their space. That isn't true for me… Cheri understands my anxiousness and is respectful and helpful in creating a safe space. Today she shared how hard of a time her middle daughter is having since COVID interrupted their lives. Cheri is incredibly understanding and patient. I often learn from her and admire how sensibly she approaches problems—head-on and always with compassion, sometimes fire. Her daughter is struggling, afraid to go out of the house lest she catches the virus and dies. In Cheri's daughter's mind, she knows that this isn't a legitimate fear, not for her, not in her own yard. Still, it's hard to convince the body it is safe when alarm bells keep ringing. The key is to regulate the alarm system. No shame, no blame. I make a mental note to pray.

Mrs. Backlund

Afterwards, I found Grace in her room hard at work. I had a few minutes before I was to interview Kristina. "How are you doing, Grace?" She seemed a bit better, more encouraged today. I am concerned for her because of the many stressors in her life. She is so responsible, and it's hard to let go of some of what she currently has little or no control over.

She had an open Social Studies book in her hands. A yellow sticky note with numbers attached to one of the pages. "Hey, would you mind making me one copy of this?" She continued explaining what was needed. I hadn't yet made copies of textbook pages, but I thought I could figure it out. When I arrived at the office, Angie was at the front desk. I waited. Most people don't. The office counter is long enough for two people, but the problem is it's narrow and hard to respect the guideline for distancing. Again, most people are okay with quickly brushing past or being comfortable three feet away. When she noticed me, she smiled and moved over. She was on her way to the photocopier. Hmmm… my brain thought. I was supposed to be meeting with Kristina now. Since Angie was already using that space, I wondered, would she mind doing this quick little job for me? I asked. Of course, she didn't.

"I'll try." She smiled and then laughed. "I'm not sure I know how. I've never done this before." Really? I was surprised and admitted, "Me neither! I was hoping you knew." "Nope, but I will figure it out." Off she went, but before I was able to leave, Grace appeared. Uh, oh… caught!

"Karen! Did you make Angie do your work?!" She admonished me in good humour. The three of us laughed. I laughed much harder a few seconds later when Angie brought out the completed task. Angie is so smiley, and always happy to help others. The trouble was that darn yellow paper I hadn't consulted. It listed many more pages in need of photocopying. What was the most amusing about my silly mistake was Grace's exaggerated exasperation? She shook her head and laughed. "I think you make mistakes on purpose, so you don't have to do jobs like this," she teased. How nice to see Grace more at ease. She has the most beautiful smile. It totally transforms her whole demeanour. It sparkles, warm and fun.

I was glad my absentminded brain produced a chuckle from her. For myself, grateful I can sometimes laugh at my missteps, trusting that my mistakes are given grace. Grace is aptly named. Later, as I was about to leave, Grace instructed with a note of excitement in her voice, "Wait! You have to follow me first." She moved quickly down the hall and out the door. A lightness in her step and in her spirit. A box for me, more 'just in case' supplies. Treats, staples, and one roll of something much coveted by the masses, toilet paper. My heart felt warm and fuzzy.

April 23 – Miss Kristina Black

Miss Black's time is precious without enough moments in a day. It would be perfectly understandable to have strict structures in place regarding her time and availability. Yet, this is so not who she is. She leads by example, with grace and purpose. I think one of her most significant assets and endearing qualities is how generous and approachable she is, always.

This afternoon we met in her office so she could share some of her thoughts on this last chaotic month. It was so odd to sit in the chair that was farthest away—duly noted by both of us. It felt weird, uncomfortable, and unnatural; a contradiction; an honest, vulnerable, close conversation, separated by two metres of space. We commiserate on how difficult it is for those of us whose love language is touch. Our instinct to move closer, is now a misstep. Another once embraced in love, is now self-distanced in fear.

Miss Black lightened the mood by describing a funny meme of what a grocery store visit looks like in today's world. How timid, suspicious, and frightened we are of others. The meme was of a kitten running around a corner and putting on the breaks as it spotted another kitten. The kitty's eyes are big, and its fur is standing on edge. Kristina giggled at the thought, using her body, hands and face to mimic the scene. Delighted and highly amused at the image of herself and other shoppers these days. Peaking around every aisle before venturing down a path laden with dangerous obstacles. Laughter is a good antidote for many ills. Proverbs says, *"A cheerful heart is good medicine, but a broken spirit saps a person's strength"* (Proverbs 17:22, NLT). I think this is Miss black's life motto. She is a great believer and cheerleader of others.

The word that kept coming up during our discussion is *big!!!* It describes well all that needs doing, the enormity of the change, the uncertainty, and the constant swirly activity in the brain. Having to reign in her legitimate feelings and emotions is... *Big...* All of it is big and unknown. In Miss Black's words, "It is a brand-new unprecedented time for which there is no model." Miss Black tries to keep calm, reassuring, and upbeat. No matter how tired or under the weather she may be, she brings her best to work each day. The bubbles about her may not be quite as bubbly, but there is still no lack or lost lustre. The effect is still light and ease, laughter, used as a way to diffuse uneasiness.

Another huge asset is her ability to multitask and easily maneuver the interweb :) Her days have been long, as they have for all the teachers. She gives herself the small luxury of sleeping in. Her daily schedule: 8:30 a.m. to 4:30 p.m. She is primarily at her desk trying to contact parents, child services, or dealing with other necessary correspondence. When not on the phone, she is answering never-ending emails. A supper break is followed by continued work on the computer. Often, she finds herself trying to return one more email at 11:00 pm. One becomes two, and before she knows it, the clock strikes midnight, and she realizes she must get herself to bed. Her head instructs her to go into survival mode; prioritize, pace, and breathe. Her heart remains aware of responsibilities, cares, and concerns that have to wait or be let go of.

Friday, March 13, two days after the WHO announced a global pandemic. Miss Black was just as much in the dark about school closures as the rest of us. An emergency district meeting instructed principals to reassure their staff school wouldn't be cancelled at this point. The message was clear. A two–three-week closure wouldn't be long enough to help contain the virus. If Alberta schools closed, it would be for an indefinite period.

Saturday, the Minister of Education stood her ground. No school closure. Sunday afternoon, another district meeting. At the time, the hypothesis was that though children likely wouldn't get sick with the disease, they were potentially excellent carriers and spreaders of the germ, therefore, thought to be highly contagious and high risk to adults. Simple instructions as to how to solve the problem with good hygiene and social distancing were laid out. Wash your hands often and stay away from others. See? Simple. How on earth could both students and staff possibly stay safe and adhere to the guidelines? School leaders worked hard attempting to come up with solutions to legitimate fears and concerns. All Sunday, they persevered. At 4:30 p.m., they paused to watch the Alberta coronavirus update. Together, they listened, in complete disbelief: schools were closed to the public effective immediately.

Miss Black's thoughts came quickly as she recalled how events kept changing:

It was such a shock. Not once through the week or weekend did I have a hint of what was coming. And then, it's just go! No time to take it in because you have to move forward with a plan. In retrospect, it would have been very beneficial had they given us a few days at home with our loved ones to just breathe. Then set out an organized plan with specific details as to how we would move forward. What a difference it would have made had the Minister shown more forbearance. Our school demographic meant fewer kids have access to necessary tools. It would have made such a difference had we been able to connect families who needed electronics devices before we started virtual school. Had we even had a few days' notice, we could have done a better job ensuring all students had what they needed for at-home learning. And we could have done a better job informing them and making them aware of the supports available. We would have had time to ask good questions, 'like who needs what?' There is no sense of finger-pointing. Everything happened so fast, and everyone did the best they could in an unprecedented situation. It's hard even to know what to be frustrated about. Without question, transitioning has been challenging. By week three, almost all of our children have now had some source of electronics that allowed them to access online learning. We are having some success. We are not in a groove yet, but little by little, it will come.

I feel like the most pleasurable and favourite parts of the job have been removed. I have to keep reminding myself that the things we are able to do are making a difference. Not in the same way, but there are things we can do. There are a few families we have not had contact with yet. I worry about many of them, and September is a long way away. It is very hard to let go of control and trust that they will be okay.

One concern is for two of our children who lost a parent a year ago. The anniversary of that date is approaching. If they were in school, we could monitor how they were doing. Our physical presence of checking in with them, staying a bit closer, would help. We can't. Physical isolation is... how do I put into words how large this need is, to take comfort, just to have another close by? I think it's important to remember the gravity of this for our little loners. Our natural way of being isn't isolated, it only feels that way, and it's a result of some type of soul injury. (I wonder at this... hmm)

The school has been pouring care into twenty food delivery boxes delivered weekly to our Avondale families. The job of connecting with all 154 parents is continuous. It takes great patience and persistence to keep trying when the many previous attempts have gone unanswered. There are many supports available for parents, whether academic, financial, or emotional. We appreciate and understand what a stressful time it has been and will continue to be. It is vitally essential for our students and parents to stay connected and access available resources.

For the children at risk, when they cannot contact a parent or guardian, Kristina and Jae (Principal and Vice-Principal) actually knock on doors. "We keep trying, and we keep pestering them. Who knows when one day they will answer. That's all we can do."

"In fact..." Her eyes lit up, and she excitedly transitioned into a feel-good story. "Yesterday afternoon I spotted a man at the front doors. It was a dad I have yet to meet! He came to pick up the boys' schoolwork. This is the first time we have had any contact with him, and the mom has not responded at all. When I asked how the boys were doing, he told me they are doing well and have been out riding their bikes! He even asked who to contact if they needed help with their schoolwork." Her face beamed. "This is what gives me joy and keeps me going! The successes we have may seem small, but not to me."

With age, disposition, experience and good mentoring come awareness—both a gift and a burden. Her warm and caring heart is willing to do nearly anything to help relieve the staff's pressures and stressors. Her insightful mind grappled with when and how to support her staff.

"When is it best to show them how, or relieve them of a task? Sometimes struggles overcome lead to soaring, and sometimes despair and defeat. How to know when it's time to simply listen or to act? Sometimes we just need to vent our frustrations."

It is a lot. It is *big* to be caring. The job is much simpler if you can break it down into a business. The trouble, and the beauty, is that it is so much more than a business in schools like ours. So much is outside the realm of our control. How do we support each other through all of this? Kristina and I discussed the need to shift our thinking.

"Instead of thinking, "*only* five children have responded," think, "*five* children have responded!" We have to, on the one hand, lower our expectations, and on the other hand, press upon ourselves and the children the possibilities of what is, not what was. This is our 'now' reality. "I haven't figured out how to have appropriate expectations for our kids. What is fair? I don't want to overwhelm those who are already feeling like this new way of being is too much. Yet, some will thrive with proper structures and some sense of routine. So many diverse needs."

"My brain hurts every day." The cure: "I laugh and go for bike rides every day with Riley. It is nice to see the sun, but the snow was actually helpful in hunkering down those first few weeks." Again, she laughed with good humour. "Never in my life have I had to answer 'I don't know' as much as I have this past month! Or, had the answer I thought I knew keep changing!"

Miss Black admitted she too feels low at times. "There have been times when a big part of me wanted to cocoon at home, stay safe and warm in my bed." She has a personal life. There are people outside of school she loves and misses, people she is concerned for, helpless to support in the ways she is accustomed. We touched briefly on Alison. How hard it was to tell the staff. There was no good way. Beyond that, is the fact that Kristina can't go visit her friend Alison or care for her in ways she (Kristina) is best at. Make her laugh, make her talk...

Her mom is starting to tire at the loneliness and absence of delight in physically being with her grandchildren. Kristina's travel plans to visit her family over Easter break had to be cancelled. Besides longing to see her mom and stepdad, and dad and stepmom, she was disappointed that she wouldn't get to see her sister's family, especially her young nephew. There are few things more desirable than having a baby respond to you in recognition, wrapping your arms around their little body as you snuggle them close. Though Kristina sees her nephew regularly on FaceTime, she hasn't seen him in person for six months! "He squeals in delight at the sound of my voice. It's the greatest!" It is. I can't wait until we all get to hold our loved ones tight again.

April 24 – Staff Meeting

Once again, the focus of today's meeting was encouraging one another with 'feel good' moments of the week. Kristina started by sharing that more parents are picking up their children's weekly work. Frontier College is sending home books for their students. Some of our students have moved, so are no longer within walking distances. No trouble, a staff member will drop off the schoolwork on their way home. Avondale is so thoughtful about performing caring gestures like this— extra out-of-the-way acts of kindness.

Phyllis works in the Kindergarten classroom. With no little ones to interact with, she has had to find other jobs. She and Lorraine have been diligently organizing the back room of the library. To their surprise, they found some helpful resources. She also had a cute story to tell. Phyllis helps with the weekly food deliveries, and yesterday morning, after she dropped off the care package, she heard her name called. She turned her head and spotted one of her kiddos sitting on his bunk bed, excitedly waving at her. "Mrs. Cash, I love you!" He called out. How sweet and heartwarming.

Miss Pomeroy, never shy to contribute her thoughts, brought up a Grade Six boy. "Has anyone heard from him? I miss seeing him in the hallways. I'd love to pick his brain to hear what he has to say about all of this."

Michelle, Angie, and Kristina had a short visit with Angie's one-on-one. They were pleased to see how he made eye contact for short bursts, and how happy he was to show them his Lego creation.

Jessie's class made a music video.

Grace shared a significant victory. She held up a picture of Flipgrid. It took me a second to register what that meant. She explained before I had to think too hard. Flipgrid is another form of interaction. Setting up programs has been a challenge, yet Grace persevered and found a way that works for her. The kids can now video themselves complimenting the student of the day. She showed an example of Jenna giving Hazel a compliment. One day, I have to seriously sit down and learn or engage myself in this current reality of communicating and staying connected.

A small group discussion followed on Zoom. Chapter Six from Jody Carrington's book, "Kids These Days." The first question: what do you do to get someone or yourself out of hard times? It's funny how timely this question is, considering where we are. Grace shared that she believes self-care is vital to maintaining our well-being.

"When we aren't looking after ourselves, our body will demand that we do. I slept for the first three days of Easter Break. The weight of coping with it all caught up with me. We have to listen to what our body is telling us."

A point that stood out for Michelle was that it is essential to get to know kids for yourself. When September comes, it is a clean slate for everyone.

Kristina found that she was plagued by headaches each evening and wasn't sleeping very well. She brought up the point she and I had discussed yesterday. The value of time to breathe, be cared for, and care for before being deposited onto the hamster wheel.

Another question led to how we express ourselves. The Five Love Languages. It has been tricky to find the way into the heart of one child. Kristina had to prod along, patient and curious. It has taken a long time, and the traditional methods she had counted on in the past weren't working. Not until she showed a genuine interest in Peyton's passion for Undertale did the relationship become possible. This weekend Kristina plans to crochet an Alphys.

When Sara feels overwhelmed, she talks. She finds a colleague to confide in or vent to. I am glad she shares what she is feeling or struggling with. It means she knows she's not alone. She misses the support of Mrs. Bailey, who is her EA. She had never worked with an EA and appreciated having another adult in the room. "It's awesome! It is great to have someone tell me it's going to be alright, or I did the right thing."

Mrs. Sandy Bailey

Sadly, I didn't get a chance to talk to Sandy face-to-face, another staff member with a beautiful smile, heartwarming and endearing. Sandy is a single, active, busy mom to three children. Pre-COVID, that is. Life is much different now. She shared a few of her thoughts with me through a text.

> Before all this, I never knew how I depended on my social life to get me through my days, but having to social distance and seclude ourselves has made me super sad and feel alone even though I know I'm not. I am slowly learning that I'm okay and don't always need to be around people. I'm finding myself wanting to improve and be better, while trying to guide my kids through these strange times. I find we are closer and have a lot of laughs and good memories together.
>
> I truly miss Avondale, the kids and especially the staff. But I'm realizing that this may be a great opportunity for me to self-reflect and maybe find another route for work and a new passion. Life is truly different but not in all bad ways, some are

very positive changes, and I'm enjoying the time I am getting with my kids.

Reading this puts a lump in my throat. And another note of realism. Sandy is kind and fun and thoughtful. Life of late, is difficult. That's the thing… we can't take away the troubles and sorrows of those we care about, but when we at least see and interact with them at school, we have some measure of comfort that our words and actions matter. It can be small acts of kindness—a door opened, a cheerful "Good morning!" a smile, a word, a hug. It can be more substantial—a burden shared, a listening ear, a caring heart, or a safe place. If Sandy doesn't return to Avondale, how much support will she lose? It saddens me because I know how much I will miss her. I love her spontaneity and her laugh. Her eyes are full of life.

"I love you, Sandy. Thanks for sharing, and you're right, it does sometimes feel like we are alone, but we are not."

"I love you too, Karen, thank you." This feels suspiciously like goodbye.

"Make sure you keep in touch every once in a while, and please let me know if you are planning to move away from Grande Prairie."

"Yes, I sure will."

"Will she?" I sure hope so. I know how easy it is for people to lose touch in our busy world.

Me

I shared I am learning to acknowledge what I am feeling, and journalling helps me process. I pray and try to focus on what I can do, not what I can't, and, as an afterthought, I added that I talk to people. This isn't entirely true. Sometimes I speak freely. Sometimes I hold on, unsure of my words or their place. It's why writing is so helpful and nourishing. My fingers have no limitations, offering no guard for my thoughts or feelings. They are highly expressive and move on their own accord. My mind will often want to edit, influence, pause, or reflect, which makes my fingers anxious. They need to move, to be known.

This is one of those moments I didn't see coming. This is painful. I haven't shared the depth of pain, sorrow, and helplessness I am feeling. I could. I don't. My head says what I am sharing is not appropriate... my spirit, though, knows I need to help myself. I need to: allow; grieve; mourn; wail. My mother is going to die soon. COVID... I can do nothing. I can take some comfort. Because my mom has dementia, she is unaware of its threat. Have the once familiar and comforting faces of the home-care nurses become disturbing? Masked and hidden... is she afraid? Confused? At times, she is defiant. It's good and bad. It means her spirit isn't defeated, but it also means she refuses to eat or drink and spits out what is good for her.

Mrs. Stephanie Marshall

I have a soft spot in my heart for Mrs. Marshall, who shares the same first name as my daughter. She is gifted in so many ways. She is always seeking knowledge and studying hard to enhance her education and teaching skills. Stephanie has had to move classrooms four times in seven years. The learning spaces she has created have been simply beautiful, serene, and tranquil. Her students excel. She is engaging and cognizant of the most current teaching principles. She is exceptionally good at being aware of volunteerism and getting involved in social reforms.

We, her fellow staff members, have benefited often because of her forward-thinking, preparedness, and thoughtfulness. Showers for babies or weddings are planned with great care and no lack of expense on her part. She believes in doing her best. If ever Stephanie decided to stop teaching, she would be a great event planner! For now, we get to keep her. Her return to Avondale will be slightly delayed by the arrival of a beautiful bundle of joy in late June or early July! We are desperately hoping some restrictions have been lifted by then. If not to hold the baby, at least to swoon over him and his mama.

Stephanie describes how she is feeling, "HUGE and overwhelmed with all of this craziness. I wish it would end already, especially from the oilfield wife's point of view where we are struggling with career and oilfield prices on top of the COVID crisis. I find having this university course to work on helps distract me on days where it becomes difficult. I'm glad you found something to give you peace in all of this."

Though I am enjoying getting to know others and capture their stories on paper, I admit it is not always a peaceful process!

April 27 – Mrs. Sue Wilson
"BE AWARE, STAY SAFE, FOLLOW THE RULES"

The message above is provided by Mrs. Wilson, who has strong convictions on how we as a society need to protect ourselves and others from the threat of COVID-19. "In the weeks to come, the people who already are very aware of following the guidelines will have to become even more aware, because the people who aren't that aware or are bending the rules, will become less careful."

Most of today's visit is centred around the effect of COVID-19— how difficult it is or has been, to maneuver ourselves safely through the various situations, whether mental health struggles, boredom, work, or physical distancing.

Sue has worked as an EA for nineteen years and is a wealth of knowledge, with endless stories to tell, some cute, some sad. She finds much to be amused at and is a good source of sensibility. At work, she is both practical and whimsical. Sue would deny and laugh at my usage of whimsical and think it not quite fitting. Having witnessed her search Pinterest for children's crafts or her own enjoyment or interest, I would say yes, she is, and that it's a lovely quality. I also appreciate how organized she is at planning and anticipating needs. As we reminisced about working together in Preschool, a picture of her came to mind. It made me smile. To respond to children physically, she would stand on her knees, so she was the same height. She could even walk on her knees. It was impressive! She laughed at herself and said, "It's just easier than bending down." Either way, it's sweet. She is patient and even-tempered, predictable. And her voice, kind. She wants children to have fun while they learn.

Loss and challenges have strengthened her and helped her be mindful of the present. Enjoy each day, moment by moment. She has been intentional about reaching out, checking in on friends and coworkers alike. I appreciate her thoughtfulness and care, and I am blessed to call her my friend.

"How do you do it, not see people hardly at all? I have my husband and kids, and still, I find it hard." Sue is very social and misses the everyday interactions with staff members. She likes hearing about others' lives and sharing what's happening in her own. "Another thing I am struggling with is trying to work from home at the same time as help my daughter with her schoolwork." They are both learning how to navigate unfamiliar situations.

Four days after the post-pandemic announcement, EAs were given the option to work at school or work from home. Sue's underlying health issues are always a reminder of how she has to carefully protect herself from potential health hazards. Now, she had to be even more aware. Working at home gave her the best chance at staying safe. Yet even in her own home, she has to rely on her husband to also be careful about social distancing and hygiene. She has to question friends she has known for years. "Are they safe? Will they remember to stay two metres away from me?"

"If I get it (coronavirus), I will probably die. I think I was probably being overly dramatic as there are only five cases in Grande Prairie... Though we don't really know," she stated, but with a slight question mark in her voice. Did I think she was overly dramatic? No, I didn't. I think she has a reason for concern. She may not die if she becomes infected, but she likely would become very sick, and that's a scary thought. We both feel the need to follow the guidelines closely. We don't want to be the person who, for whatever reason, passes the virus to another.

Sue is so responsible and forward-thinking that she has been consciously keeping track of all the people she comes in contact with, just in case. The task was made easier by limiting her outings. At home, life gets boring. Too much television, not enough book reading or knitting. "It sucks!" she exclaimed. "I do still have virtual house parties, though." She laughed. She likes to laugh and have fun with her friends and is diligent in making it happen. Three times a week, they get together to play games. I admire how intentional she is about staying connected and interactive with others.

News watching is a normal part of Sue's day. Often at lunchtime, she would relay interesting bits on current events. When the news broke, she wasn't taken by surprise by the impending threat to our livelihoods. Returning relatives from Panama didn't quarantine upon returning, so she had to ban them from visiting. At times she feels grouchy. Don't we all. COVID has hampered and restricted much. I know we are fortunate in many ways, but this crisis has undoubtedly brought about challenges. There are conflicting, different points of view about risks and management. Some of it is simply a lack of understanding or conflicting interpretations of what our health experts are telling us. Some are in denial, oblivious, or impervious. Others may claim they are rational and laid back.

Sue found the first staff meeting unsettling. Well informed, Sue chose a seat as far away from others as possible. Though social distancing was in the news, many people hadn't been following its progress. No cases in Grande Prairie. No worries. No one seemed to notice Sue's attempt at social distancing. She was brave and honest when Stacy approached.

"Please don't. I am trying to respect the distancing guideline." Stacy immediately found another seat. However, most of the staff didn't get how serious things were and thought she was joking. One staff member thought she would make the joke funnier by sitting right next to her. Days later, when social distancing was front and centre in every newscast, she realized how her actions might have been perceived as inappropriate. Sincerely sorry for making Sue uncomfortable, she apologized. She simply hadn't been aware of how contagious and dangerous the virus was. No one on our staff would purposely make another feel threatened.

I feel like this was another oversight by someone (Minister of Education or the School Board?) A global pandemic was declared—a once in a century occurrence—and teaching staff were required to show up the next day without proper guidelines. Had they waited a few days, they would have saved a lot of angst, indecisiveness, and confusion. Their lack of preparedness and direction led to a lack of adequate information and awareness of the importance of social distancing.

"This is gross, but one day, the light was just right, and I could see the spit coming out of someone's mouth while they talked. Every time we laugh, cry, sneeze, cough, spit is coming out of our mouths. I had to stop going to school and out in public when I couldn't control what others did. The only way to do that is to stay home. It is hard to be a rule follower when others aren't listening. It makes me mad."

I hear her, and at times there's an internal conflict. To bend the rule or not? There are only five cases here. I'm safe. I'm six feet away. Only in some cases, I'm not. And how do I know? And, living where we are so protected, so lucky, shouldn't I do my part? Or am I too stuffy? Too paranoid? No... like Sue said, "If everyone followed the rules as closely as we do, we would be able to resume normal life much sooner."

Even when she tries to bend the rules, she gets caught. "A few weeks ago, some of my friends and I met in an empty parking lot. We stayed in our vehicles and socially distanced. A bylaw officer stopped and told us we had to go. He said it's kind of a grey area. Not only that, but a friend of mine also had a fire pit in her front yard. We are kind of allowed front yard visits, so I thought I would do the same... no, permit says only back yard."

While Sue has a serious side, she also has a sense of humour and easily finds ways to amuse herself. After packing up the Grade-Six classroom, she neatly displayed their bags of belongings in the gymnasium in the shape of a flower! She had a great big grin on her face as she told me about the display she made. "You should have seen it! It was hilarious!" she chuckled.

April 28

On a somewhat difficult day, a piece of welcoming news. Friends can start getting together outside in small groups. I miss my friends. I still can't see my grandsons with social distancing in place. But to have a friend sit on my deck for a cup of tea, how nice, normal... and needed.

I spoke with my mom's doctor today, and though her condition hasn't changed, it was comforting to know how kind and caring her doctor is. Though my mom is frail, her vital organs are functioning well for her age. She simply doesn't want to eat or drink or be.

9:30 pm

I don't want to simply endure this time in history, or waste any of it feeling left out or cheated. Or be guilty of killing time with endless hours of television and inactivity. This time in my life matters as much as any other time, and is precious, even if most of it is spent alone.

Funny how we all have these different ways of coping. Often, we recognize the absurdity and can laugh at ourselves. This morning, Grace said she was up at midnight baking buns! When her husband asked her why, she responded with a very logical response, "There was a bun starter in the fridge."

Mrs. Michelle Elliott

An hour earlier, while visiting with Mrs. Elliott, our Learning and Early Literacy support teacher, she commented on something similar to what Grace had said. She has found herself 'chippy,' a term proliferated by Jody Carrington. She was angry at some small thing; a small thing/big reaction moment. She laughed while telling me about the thing that set her off, musing: "It's not unfamiliar to us. It's just that usually we see it in the children we work with. It is us reminding them to consider the size of the problem. The problem is not the small thing, it is the thing you can't escape. Even when it is not hitting you directly, it still impacts or hinders your behaviour and movements. Take this COVID thing, for example... let us count the ways."

Michelle is an upbeat person, sensible and insightful. She has a great deal of the common sense and calmness needed to respond well and be supportive and reasonable with herself, her family, and her job: staff, parents, and students. She has a willingness to do whatever needs doing and an understanding of what can wait, with an insight into prioritizing—what comes first? What can she do? Is this something she has control over? Crucial skills to utilize, and the opportunities to use them abound.

That Friday (March 13), I remember talking to Kristina about the possibility of schools being closed. We both thought, 'No way, not possible, too much impact on too many people.' I wasn't worried or concerned. Sunday, we had about thirty people over for my son's year-end hockey party. We had a fire. Kids were skating and roasting hot dogs. It was great. Then, about three of us got a series of beeps on our phones from the CBC app. I couldn't believe it. I thought, 'Holy Crap!'

Even now, as she remembers the moment, she is visibly heightened, animated in her telling. Looking at the invisible phone in her hand. "All of us parents were like, 'What does this mean?' The kids were oblivious to it all until I used my teacher's voice. You know, the stern one that alerts kids you have something important to say. '*Stop!* I have something to tell you. There is no school on Monday. Schools are being closed to the public.' The kids threw up their gloves like they won a big game, hooped and hollered."

Her daughter didn't take the news well. As a Grade Twelve student, it's hard to collect all the disappointments and challenges they must be feeling. "My poor daughter, I must have spent an hour trying to console her. Most every question she asked, I couldn't answer. 'How long? What about grad diplomas?' It was crazy!"

"No one knew. My daughter has worked so hard to catch up so she can finish Grade Twelve with her classmates. Having a baby at fifteen is hard. She has had to make many sacrifices."

I love how caring and heartfelt Michelle was as she spoke of her daughter. She was proud of the work and sacrifices her daughter has made over the last few years. Empathetic to what a blow this is. Some things we don't readily think about for many young people graduating. Those special moments… the dress… Michelle's daughter's dress sits in a closet altered and ready to go… just in case.

"Concern for my family's well-being overshadowed work. Work was crazy anyway, not knowing what to do. Everything is so different." Michelle's family also includes her visiting parents. They come for a visit every winter and have their own suite in the basement. Her father is seventy-five, and her mom seventy-three. Her mom has emphysema, so she is at higher risk if she were to contract coronavirus. Her mom hasn't entirely grasped how serious this is, how careful she needs to be. At first, they thought they would go home to Newfoundland, but with her mom's compromised immune system and airports being the most dangerous place, it wasn't a viable option.

"What I remember about the first day back at school is noticing all the cleaning people. Everywhere and everything is disinfected. My hands were so sore from using so much sanitizer. It was an almost panicked feeling. Not panic, but scared." She searched for the appropriate adjective for what she felt. She couldn't quite grasp the mixture of emotions in a word.

"Everything was happening so fast, and there were reminders all around that said, 'CLEAN CLEAN CLEAN!' I quickly became very vigilant about cleaning in my own area."

We agreed on the varying levels of acceptance people seem to have. It was something Michelle noticed in the first few weeks of coming to school. What motivates us to choose one way or another? We contemplated those who don't heed the guidelines, not the 'just bend the rule a little' people. Do they just not care? Or is it a way of denying the threat? For her, her parents are her number one reason for carefully adhering to guidelines. She doesn't fear for herself, but what if she contracted the virus and passed it on to them?

As with the rest of us, her job description has temporarily been adjusted. Cognizant of how overwhelmed many of our parents are, she hasn't sent home the extra instruction she typically supplies. Not yet. They have enough new things to absorb. The most important thing parents can do is encourage their kids to read every day for fifteen or twenty minutes. She has been calling parents, trying to encourage them and make them aware of the different ways Avondale School is still available to support them. We understand how tough this is.

"It can be frustrating not getting a hold of people, leaving messages that don't get returned. I want to say to each family, "Haven't forgotten about you, just need to hear your voice. There is not much we can do about getting to see them until the kids say they want to see us." Her demeanour alters slightly for a few seconds, that feeling that isn't resigned or giving up but wishing you could change attitudes; the need to get through, so you know the kids are okay.

"I have been doing more things like trying to support the teachers, especially Brittany. I had just written up all of the kids' IPP's for next year as they are going into Grade 7. I was able to supply background information and some helpful tips on how to connect with some of the kids. I have found a few good webinars that I have helped Mrs. Thomson with. She is doing well at learning new programs. Also, I have been helping to set up and deliver food. That's been good because I now know where some of them live." She said this with a sly smile and twinkle.

"I am a very visual person. What has been really helpful for me are the Jody Carrington podcasts. Each morning I come to work, I turn on the smartboard and listen specifically for one or two things I can focus on. A word or a phrase. A quote. I write them on my board where I can see them, and then, when I'm feeling mentally drained, I am reminded to check in with myself, lower my shoulders, breathe. Jody has lots of helpful advice, such as: "We are 'crisis schooling,' not homeschooling." If we look through this lens, our priorities and expectations are more likely to match reality and be more effective. I have used her advice to encourage and counsel parents who are concerned with what is happening with their kid's learning.

Routines and structures are foundational for Michelle's well-being. She was sensible in realizing how important it was to build a new routine quickly. Though her home was full of family, she needed to come to school and see her coworkers. "The connection in this building is huge! And there have been enough safe practices put in place that I am comfortable being here." It is true. And as each day draws closer to April 30, the 'swept under the rug' thoughts of, "What will happen to each of us? Where will we be? The comfort of having others drop by to say hi, gone…" poke out.

Walking is another measure Michelle has woven into her routine. "I find walking reflective. It is good for both mental and physical health." This is interesting, and I want to know more.

"What do you reflect on?" I ask, curious. I don't work closely with Michelle. We don't see much of her in the lunchroom. In general, she always seems like she's in a good mood, staying calm but firm dealing with challenging behaviours.

"I reflect on what I am learning, what I would do differently, what I do next. It teaches me. I like growing. I am mindful of the need for self-care. Walking is part of that."

She smiles at the thought of an ulterior motive and added pleasure. "I watch for students when I'm walking. Are they outside playing? Looking for signs they are doing okay. I saw Bradly and Brayden and visited with them for about fifteen minutes." She is pleased and has a plan.

"Each day, I look forward to maybe seeing them again. I wonder if I need to change my route, so I see more kids."

April 30 – Mrs. Backlund

My last day with Grace is both lovely and melancholy. While Grace works away at the weekly plan and virtual teaching, I assemble the paper material into homework packages. My mind, tired, is lulled and steadied by the simple act of stapling, sorting and counting, and listening to Grace talk through her ideas. Occasionally she asks a question she knows I can't answer. I know she knows, and I know she isn't expecting an answer; it's merely comforting to have another in the room, working apart but together. Occasionally we stop to comment or laugh at something. Lunchtime nears, and Grace declares, "We need cupcakes!" Off she goes to buy us a delicious treat for our last day. Neither of us wants to acknowledge this last day… what it means…

Once she returns, we toast our year, the year we will never forget—light, easy banter with chocolate and icing. For a moment, our faces turn serious. Does she want to share for the journal?

"I can't even find words to use to articulate my feelings. How can I talk about my trauma when I am still in the middle of it? I can't even begin to process, and I don't know when I will ever have the time to."

My heart feels for Grace. She is right, she can't let any air out, or she risks completely deflating. I wish Grace could see that she is succeeding, despite how she feels or how long everything takes to prepare or accomplish. It doesn't seem fair how hard she has to work at everything. I admire that, despite how overwhelmed Grace is, she keeps showing up—giving the best of what's available to give.

Despite the losses and uncertainties, I don't want anything to be wasted in my experiences. It isn't easy, but it is doable, and there are moments to hold. I cannot change or stop whatever may come. My job is to adapt... trust... search for... and to have eyes to see and ears to hear. I am under no illusion that everything is or will be without sacrifice, unease, or pain. Always I have a choice as to how I am going to respond. I have adopted the definition of 'thrive' a friend of mine shared with me recently. To 'thrive' is to grow and develop.

April 30

The day was odd. We grouped whenever possible. Reluctant to leave each other. The two permanent aids bemoaned the fairness of us with temporary contracts getting laid off. They encouraged, "We will all be back. There will be a need for us." Two other permanents, on loan from another school, start work at Avondale on Monday. What does that mean for us? "Of course, you will have jobs." The reality is, nobody knows for sure.

We met on Zoom for our farewell staff meeting and a chance to say, 'goodbye for now and thank you for your service.' Mrs. V.'s smart-board was on, making our faces and expressions more transparent. There was room in her class for several of us to gather safely. I fetched Mrs. Troyer so she could be with me, Mrs. Thomson, and Mrs. V. As usual, Miss Pomeroy and Ms. Kay entertained the rest of us by regaling stories and sharing funny memes. As each staff member popped up on the screen, I noticed, that though most were smiling, their eyes were sad or sombre, tender. The main screen kept changing, and an enlarged picture of a staff member would briefly take centre stage. Mrs. Bailey was at home in her PJs. I miss her. I haven't seen her in person since the last day the kids were in school. She looks so young. I wonder how she is. Sara urged Mrs. Marshall to show us how much her baby is growing. Stephanie's blue eyes and lovely dimples, subdued. Miss Stokes is thoughtful in her gaze. Mrs. Quinn was caring and empathetic as she watched the screen.

Sara serenaded us with a song. "I will remember you…" Kristina laughed, boisterous, and in merry amusement exclaimed, "I love it!"

Jae's computer background—a beach with a palm tree. It looked inviting.

Jesse, ever the ham, cleverly kept changing her computer background screen, making sure it was interesting enough to capture our attention, thus diverting us from feeling sad.

Miss Black and Mrs. LeClerc shared their gratitude for each of us. We are a big part of Avondale's success and an essential part of the family. They will miss us. With sincere caring and warmth, Miss Black thanked each EA.

Mrs. Wilson: "I was thrilled when an opportunity arose last year to hire Sue back. You have such compassion for children. I love seeing you with them walking up and down the hallways!"

Mrs. Bailey: "Sandy, you had such a challenging job, I don't know if I have ever seen a kid with more complex needs. Thank you for always being willing to learn." Sara jumped in, "I honestly don't know what I would have done without you. I love you, man!"

Mrs. Tollefson: "Cheyenne, I am not sure how you do what you do with such grace on a daily basis. You exude patience and understanding. You are an inspiration to me. You are so young, yet so wise. It has been a privilege working and learning from you."

Mrs. Quinn: "Not only is Stacy one of the moms we count on, but also a mom to our students in how she takes them under her wings. I appreciate how she would bring immediate concerns for kids to my attention. She has great instincts, especially for our more complex students. And thank you for never rolling your eyes, well, at least not in front of me, when asked to work in a different capacity." A bit of laughter erupted.

Ms. Powell: "You have such insight into people's hearts and so often understand the roots behind behaviours. I see that even more with the writing you are doing. Thank you."

Mrs. Jody: "What stands out the most to me is the work you have done with Biannca. And each time Biannca has success, the joy on your face is wonderful! I admire your compassion and ability to connect with children."

Mrs. Cash: "Phyllis, you have brought your warm, wonderful qualities to the kindergarten classroom. It is evident in everything you do how much you care about the students in your care. It was especially wonderful to see you bond with Cody and how you would do anything to ensure he was at school and learning to the best of his ability. Thank you for your service to our students."

Mrs. Troyer: "You are a rock star! You have an amazing work ethic! You are always the supportive and positive one. You are always thinking of not just the kid in your class but of their brother or sister too. Blows me away: that you make an extra craft for the sibling. Your sense of calm radiates, always you instill the sense of, 'We got this!' And great insight." Mrs. Marshall added her appreciation for how helpful Cheri has been getting all the packages together, but more for being a safe, supportive friend. "You're the best."

I glanced across the room, hoping to catch Cheri's eye. She is all of those things and more. Mrs. V. thoughtfully walked across the room and offered Cheri a tissue.

Jae made a toast, and we raised our glasses. This is not goodbye, though you wouldn't have known it by our faces, save a few, the ones who do their best to lighten the mood. Afterwards, Cheri quietly slipped away. I waited a few minutes and then walked down the hall. Cheri is one of the kindest and tender-hearted people I know. Tears are (usually) kept at bay. I met Mrs. Thomson coming out of Cheri's classroom. She had the same thought as I and took the chance to say goodbye. As I walked in, Cheri was blowing her nose, her eyes still red, tears recently wiped away. I had this second of wanting to draw closer. A natural instinct—to welcome or encourage in an embrace. I caught myself leaning in and stepped back. Cheri found her chair behind the desk. I found one six to eight feet away.

"I just got myself together when Mrs. Thomson stopped by, now you." She sighed. "I never cry. I don't know why I am."

Appreciation and kind words are reminders of her place and role in our school. Cheri was letting herself feel the loss of the present and perhaps the loss of the future. Almost always, she outwardly conveys strength and is dependable and supportive. She works hard and keeps upbeat. Today's spotlight on her tugged at a thread. The ball of yarn inside, not messy or tangled or about to unravel, but loosened...

Ms. Jessie Kay

The first room I peeked into this morning was Ms. Kay's. I was met with familiar, welcoming, mischievous blue eyes. Her trademark long hair hung loosely today. She was visiting with Mrs. Quinn. In her hand, she held a cup of Tim Horton's coffee. I joked, "Where's mine?" Last year, when we worked in the same classroom, at least once a week, she brought me a coffee. Without batting an eye, she nodded to the familiar shelf where I had kept my drinks. There sat coffee! Somehow, though pleased, I wasn't surprised.

So outgoing, involved, and interactive, it is hard to believe Ms. Kay was painfully shy as a child. Now she seems forthcoming and honest in expressing her feelings. When she is frustrated, she lets you know, but most often, it seems she rebounds quickly from setbacks. She is quick-witted, and always has a quip or response. Sends funny memes for amusement. She is known as a fun, creative teacher. The kids appreciate that she treats them like big kids. She jokes with them and spends extra time at building relationships at the end of the day after the school bell rings. COVID-19 has changed her approach to teaching. In one of our early staff meetings, I remember her commenting, "This whole new way of doing things goes against everything I believe in. I am all about organic, hands-on learning."

Later that day, we sat down together so I could interview her. Our conversations are always interesting. Jesse tries hard to be mindful, open-minded, and respectful of other people's points of view. She isn't easily swayed or biased by her personal beliefs. Often, we have the same thought in our heads. I can read what she hasn't said, and sometimes even what she isn't letting herself feel. She is aware of her emotional makeup. Though she is open and honest, she tends to lighten tense atmospheres with humour—case in point, the attractive picture of Tom Selleck on her screen during our staff meeting.

Other interviews have lasted between thirty minutes and one hour, but today's took almost three. True, we were interrupted four times, but even so, we haven't had many chances throughout the year to sit together and share, and we don't want to rush through. Ms. Kay is a very good talker. I mean that in the best way: engaging, funny, thoughtful, and earnest.

She said she'd been putting me off for the last two weeks. Yes, she wanted to share. The trouble is she had so much to say. Not just say but feel. At times, it's difficult to name or own our feelings. COVID-19 demands a response. It isn't sympathetic to our infirmities, impositions, losses, comfort, or plans. Its presence may not loom large overall, but its breath blows harsh and cold, and not one of us is allowed to be indifferent. Ms. Kay knows this is true.

Mrs. Quinn, who has worked all year in Jessie's class, is just leaving but won't say goodbye. Each of us will text. We will visit, stay connected. This isn't goodbye. It has been difficult all day to hold our composure, to ignore the fact that for eight of us, this is our last day of work… for this year… and maybe, ever.

Finally, we were ready to start. Jessie is… Jessie… charming in every way. She is endearing with an ever-present smile and twinkle in her eyes. The sparkle doesn't always infer joy, only that she is engaged— in wonder, awe, laughter, or righteous indignation. She made herself comfortable and began.

The hardest part for me was the week of March 9–13. I had been listening to the news, so I knew what was going on. You know me, I like to use humour to mask my feelings, but Mrs. Quinn and I, and even the kids, were feeling suspicious. We had a couple of sick kids in our classroom and a couple who had travelled. We had a sub who had just returned from the states. And one or two teachers had recently returned from outside of Canada. All of January and February, both students and teachers were sick. I only had thirty percent of my kids show up in January and only sixty percent in February. It is just the weirdest and strangest feeling to be suspicious. Coronavirus was the buzzword all week. Kids talked non-stop about it. Attuned to adult conversations at home, on the news, and in the school environment, the kids were picking up on both the spoken and unspoken message of the need to be wary. It was startling to notice how they seemed to be gravitating away from those who were sick. We (the adults) were worried too. How careful did we have to be? Thoughts of, 'hey, they shouldn't be here.'

Ms. Kay's face and voice grew even more animated as she shared. It's remarkable how impressionable that day was in her mind, still so vivid in the retelling. "It was unknown and alarming. What was coming might be nothing, but it also could be huge. It was all the kids could talk about."

I felt the same about our classroom. I felt a heightened sense of unrest and, for lack of a better word, pre-pandemic panic. Like Mrs. Backlund, Mrs. Kay knew she needed to address the kids' fears and misconceptions. Jessie has excellent skills with spoken words. She knows how to get to the heart of a problem, how to strike the balance of information: serious enough to have the students' full attention and also aware that they are only nine years old, still pretty little for something so big. After, she tried to explain what all this meant: wash your hands; stay away from others. You won't get sick, but your grandparents might, so you may need to stay away from them for a while. She tried to answer questions she didn't know the answers to.

"I had this really odd moment near the end of the day when the kids were getting ready to leave. Just something inside, an urge, driving me to speak out. What if? I wanted or needed to warn them. When the bell went, I called out, 'Okay, guys, if I don't see you on Monday, I miss you.' It blew my mind."

I wasn't sure just yet if she was still speaking about the first day or had moved on, so expressive were her four words.

"Some places were shutting down their schools, and some weren't. Was it really necessary?"

Humour and slightly objective distancing are the coping strategies of Ms. Kay. It isn't a bad thing in moments of crisis if it helps to accomplish what's necessary. She laughed in almost disbelief at herself as she remembered: "That first day was kind of almost fun. No kids, maybe no school. A weird combination of ominous and awe, fear and disbelief. Not terrified, but scary. I tried to keep things light for myself and others."

There is something mysterious and exciting about being a tiny bit frightened. If we know we are safe and not at risk, it can be almost tantalizing. Hearts beat faster. Adrenaline rushes. Misplaced giggles bubble. That is why people watch horror movies. Others go on scary carnival rides. The potential danger and fear have a clear start and end. For the most part, we can watch natural disasters in both empathy and fascination when they are a world away. Listening to many of our staff members, this was a partially true representation of a collective response.

"On the second day, I felt suddenly angry during our staff meeting. We were all sitting shoulder to shoulder. It felt absurd. If the situation was so serious and dramatic that we couldn't have kids in school because we couldn't keep them the required distance apart, why were we all sitting so close together?" We agreed it appeared that those in charge hadn't thought things through. They had panicked, protecting the students, but not given a lot of thought to their employees' mental or physical health. Again, not finger-pointing but rather an observation. We know everyone is doing their best, and what is needed is that we continue to seek to learn, to see where we can do better—to reflect, modify, plan and prepare for future challenges we are sure to face. Not an easy task. Ms. Kay recalled:

It made me mad to see some people not being respected and given the physical distance they asked for. One situation totally took me by surprise, my reaction intense and spoken. Emotions were high. Some people closely follow the guidelines, and some do not. And it's not even so much that I was freaked out about social distancing. It was more about respecting other people's boundaries. I don't know if some people just don't get it. And then it bugged me to hear all the talk of the most tragic events. And the way everything gets judged. People were watching the streets to see who is socially distancing and who is not. All of it was too much. I had a hard time accepting, and I started to shut down.

We both reflected and theorized on the human condition. How we each respond so differently. Ms. Kay is a good study on people, thoughtful and intuitive. "It seems like there are levels of acceptance. And I am always trying to read the other person, so I know how to be with them. It's difficult remembering who is comfortable and who is not. Some people are very conscious of social distancing."

I interjected by putting my hand up—a small poke of fun at myself. Confessing, "That's me! I have had to say, 'I need six feet!'" Though I smiled good-naturedly, I was serious. Ms. Kay countered with, "Ya, but you always have a smile on your face, and no one gets offended. You just take a step back." She moved her head back. It was amusing because she mirrored my reaction to people when they get too close to me. This led to more profound, more reflective thought. Why is it that because we don't want to hurt someone's feelings, we are put in the position of having to choose? Why let our own boundary of safety be compromised rather than risk offending someone? It's interesting. Jesse shared a Meme called Poetry of Pictures, all the faces of social distancing. This extraordinary time in history is exposing our insecurities, testing our beliefs, and stressing our working friendships.

"It is a bizarre process—for example, Google Classroom. At first, I thought it was 'Impossible.' I told Mrs. Backlund I would do simple and easy and not Google. When I got home, I was curious. I began, and thought, this is manageable. I tried one thing, and then another, and then I was motivated and into it. What is absolutely unfamiliar is this fight within, in regard to our early successes. We want to learn from each other and congratulate each other on them, yet they have also become a root of resentment. It makes you feel sick because you can't catch up. Either you feel like you don't have the ability, or your students' families don't or won't."

This is such a brilliant, astute, and honest admission, I asked that she repeat it. I wanted to write it exactly as she said it—an important truth. We love and want our friends and coworkers to succeed, yet when we feel like we are the only ones failing, we tend to go inward instead of outward. Fall back, retreat. Our eyesight dims. The brain becomes a bit foggy or discouraged—hands slower, heart heavier. We aren't meant to walk alone, and yet, why is it when we struggle, it is so hard to go to another and admit to a legitimate need for help? For understanding and support?

We have a really good rhythm going. Occasionally I add a thought of my own, a pause to catch up, but mostly there is a steady stream of intense thoughts and feelings.

"The third day, I felt pretty emotional when I learned my student teacher wasn't coming back. At times I felt almost hysteria, my emotions all over the place. Multiple personalities. Funny one moment, angry another. Overwhelmed. It was painful on my psyche."

We perhaps could have spent a few more moments here if not for the first interruption. Interruption is the wrong word; pause is a better, more accurate description. Each visitor was welcomed, as the visit was a need to see another person one last time. It's Mrs. Wilson. She kept her eyes averted and attempted to keep her voice light. To Jesse, "You made me laugh so hard at your funny backgrounds that kept changing!" Remembering, she laughed again. "I am not saying goodbye. I refuse to. This is not goodbye," a small croak in her voice.

The second interruption was less welcomed, an email from a parent.

The third pause was for Ms. Stokes. Her smile lacked lustre, a sadness in her eyes. And her body language showed the strain of this day. She asked Jessie a question about a program. The teachers have all struggled learning and accepting the challenges of virtual learning. I can't emphasize enough the long nights and angst they have endured. Dedicated and professional, they have worked hard to do more than the government's expectations. Today, though, Miss Stokes has come to a decision that I hope she sticks to. Her days have to be the same as before, meaning the number of hours she works. Jesse wants Miss Stokes to teach her the recorder along with her students. The conversation switches back to preparing lessons. The nature of preparing lessons is ridiculous.

"I had to use seven different platforms to create quality work for my kids. All that for one and a half hours of work. What used to take me five minutes to do (photocopying) now takes me forty-five minutes to two hours, just for one activity."

I am amazed every time I listen to the new language they are using, describing how to go from here to there. I'm lost, and it scares me how foreign it all is. Jesse admitted much of it has been foreign to her, and it has taken hours to learn—at the expense of time stolen from her children, a pang of guilt. Practically every moment of the day and late into the night is spent learning, creating, emailing, or talking on the telephone with a parent. In all of her seven years of teaching, she hasn't had nearly the parent communication that she's had in the last six weeks. Mrs. Leclerc poked her head in, "Got a minute?" Sure, Jessie always has time.

Jae has a program-related question. How to set up? Ms. Kay opened up her smartboard to give an example, and my heart skipped a beat. On the screen was a picture of her Grade Three class standing against the school wall. The Wolf PAC. I worked in their class last year an hour on most days, and I have a strong attachment to them. After Jae had what she needed, she headed for the door but stopped when Jesse called out, "Thank you, Jae, for always keeping calm through all of this. I know it's hard. I have to keep telling myself and parents to be patient. I am working on the answers to their questions." One thought led to another, and Jae responded, "From the start, we have been conscious of the needs of our families. First, mental health, second, food supply and delivery, and then learning."

Jessie and I continued our conversation along the same vein. So many needs. Jessie's hands become more active as she shares all the thoughts and worries she has experienced. She sought hard for the right word or phrase to describe or capture the immensity and more.

"It is not just a juggling act... it's more... I miss my students. I worry about them. Are they safe, scared, hungry? I worry about my colleagues. Are they okay? Did I say something or do something insensitive or make them uncomfortable? I worry for my partner. He was laid off and was feeling inadequate. I worry about my kids. Are they getting enough of my attention? They don't get to see their grandparents. I used to worry about my parents all the time. I worry about my grandma's mental health. I worry about our administrators. They are so strong and doing such a good job. I never stop long enough to take stock of how I am."

It is a lot to have in one's head and heart. Though I can change nothing about any of her concerns, I am glad she is sharing. She made a big circle with her hands. "It's like I have all these spikes coming out from my head, each a worry for someone. I am like the bunny from Alice in Wonderland! Running around, 'I'm Late, I'm late, I'm late! Schedule, schedule... "

There is less laughter. It's not a joke. It is how she feels. She seldom lets herself get weary or tired. She is confessing the hugeness of the load and expectations; many she has put upon herself. We both know teachers are good at being martyrs. Sometimes putting others first and focusing on their needs is a way of distracting ourselves from unresolved issues. Needing every detail to be right is a way of controlling when so little is controllable.

"I am thankful my life has not been affected very drastically. I still get to go home every night to the people I love, and the TV shows I like. The timing is amazing. If I were a first-year teacher instead of a seventh-year teacher my financial situation would be a lot less secure."

Mrs. Thomson stops to say goodbye, just from the door and without words. She didn't need them. All of her feelings were felt from thirty feet away. Her body exudes sadness. "I don't like this at all."

The clock shows it's past four o'clock. It's time to leave soon. Is there anything else Ms. Kay would like to share? Earlier, she mentioned her friend, Shawn, a friend since high school. Did she want to finish her thoughts on his death? He was one of the first young people to die in Alberta from COVID-19.

"It was the first time the actual health effects of COVID got real to me. Young people could die. It helped that his life was celebrated so much. He was a big Oilers fan, and they even made a tribute video for him. Then we waited for Grande Prairie to get hit. We thought, 'okay it's coming.' And then it didn't. Feels funny to say this, but it is almost underwhelming. And I don't want to say disappointing..."

I stepped in. I understand we don't want to experience what was happening in Italy and New York in a real sense, but when you take away the real people dying and losing loved ones, there is a fascination for most people. It doesn't make you a bad person, it's more incomprehensible to us because cases are so low. Nor does it mean those of us who are very cautious are silly and overreacting. She continued:

Remember in the beginning when the experts advised extreme measures, and everything got shut down? Wouldn't it be great if, in six weeks, it looks as though we overreacted? Means social distancing will have worked. Here we are six weeks later, and Grande Prairie only has five cases. There are some pretty smart people who think maybe the virus has already gone through Grande Prairie. We have the youngest population. Maybe we just didn't get as sick.

You know what was cool? Zachery emailed me. He was scared and didn't seem to know precisely why the school was closed. He was worried one of the teachers was sick. I emailed him back and explained why schools were closed and that we were all okay. He said thank you, and that made me feel better. We are adjusting. I think back to the first week, watching Dillon play on the playground. It made me feel disconnected, and everything so foreign. Now, three weeks later, we have created a classroom on Zoom.

It is pretty amazing how adaptable humans are. The hard work, tears and frustration, and perseverance is paying off. It isn't what anyone wants. But it is what it is, and each of us is doing the best that we can—days of up, days of down.

We did not say goodbye. A wave, see you later.

May 1

Cases in Alberta 5,355

Cases in Canada 53,236

As the process of journalling Avondale staff's initial response winds down, a theme has emerged. With each story I listened to, I gained insight and appreciation for the need to mourn losses of any kind. And whether we actively pursue or acknowledge a loss, it is there just the same. Throughout each story, there is a multitude of losses. The stages of grief follow a similar pattern—each of us is at a different place as we accept the loss. Not always do the steps stay ordered, yet they remain predictable markers of where we are in our recovery process.

The Five Stages of Grief
1. Denial or shock and isolation (the buffer)
2. Anger (deflects vulnerabilities)
3. Bargaining (rationalizing, what if's or postponing the inevitable)
4. Depression (sadness, regret, worry or/and the more subtle, private quiet preparation to separate or bid farewell)
5. Acceptance (also withdrawal but marked by calm and peace with the inevitable. It sees/acknowledges what is, what was, and asks what next?) (Elizabeth Kiiber-Ross)

May 6

God help me. I didn't see this wave of pain coming. Tears slide down my cheeks. A few things have infringed upon my peace—FaceTime with a close friend.

Though I am grateful, look forward to, enjoy, and am comforted seeing and spending time with my friend, it is a reminder that we can't see each other in person. I worry for her. What if we don't get a vaccine, and what if it is never safe to hug her again? This thought hurts my heart. I was checking school emails. Two permanent EAs from another school were transferred and welcomed to Avondale today. A surprising stab of feeling left-out needles me. Thoughts of 'not needed,' 'not able,' and 'not wanted' try to muscle their way through my vulnerable weakened state. I recognize the lies, none of them are true, and yet, I feel at risk of going inward, listening to my insecurities, not knowing what is real. Looking at my friends' faces, enjoying them, normal, and safe, and sure, I'm afraid that if I don't pursue…

Most people have full lives, and though I matter to them… it isn't quite the same as needing them to check in on me. I try to be brave. I try and I try to not need… I bite my finger. I have regrouped momentarily. No… not really… I'm in distress. Try to think mundane thoughts. The dam is breaching. It sounds dumb. My feelings are big and scary and not at all tamed or processed. I thought I evolved and was in a state of acceptance. I am not. I can't name what I am feeling. Some is a legitimate heartache—of loss, of closeness to others.

Today is Mental Health Wellness Day. Dr. Hinshaw counselled people to make sure to reach out to their close-support network and look out for those who might not tell you they are in need. I am in need. I want to change course, read my book. Will I have solved anything? Or just delayed? Or are these outbursts of painful sobbing also part of the new normal?

Earlier, while Facetiming with my friend, she reminded me to remember the reason for physical distancing, and why I am out of work, is COVID-19. Don't look too hard for more. It is enough and certainly a cause for grief. I feel calmer. Remember to breathe.

I observe. My hands are gentle as I smooth the tabs on the keyboard.

Careful and mindful, my fingers are not frantic in their race to expel, reveal, or be seen.

They are not angry in indignation, anxious, or fearful. They remain still, not tapping, and occasionally resting. I am not too sensitive or fragile. I'm human. My house is quiet and still, just me and my thoughts that aren't clear and don't need to be. They just are. This is a new experience for me. I don't know how to perceive it. Moving forward? In some respects, yes, but if I think too hard, then the calm is unsettling, detached from emotion.

I observe myself. Be still.

I am relieved and grateful. I wasn't actually detached from my emotions. I felt them, acknowledged them, owned them, and by choosing wisely, cared for myself. I have successfully navigated my age-old crisis coping strategy: be strong. Don't need. Deny painful feelings. Tumble into disordered thinking. I don't have to always be strong. It's not only okay to need, it's healthy and helps build relationships. I'm not rejected but accepted and cared for. My thinking is sound. *"For God has not given us a spirit of fear, but of power, and of love and of a sound mind"* (2 Timothy 1:7).

May 30

Cases in Alberta 6,878

Cases in Canada 99,853

As of today, there are just six cases of COVID-19 in Grande Prairie. I don't know why we've been so lucky. I am grateful. Our city has quietly gone about its business. I believe most people have tried to be careful and respectful of Alberta Health Services' guidelines. Life has become somewhat normalized as restrictions have eased. I found both Dr. Deena Hinshaw (Alberta's Chief Medical Officer), as well as Dr. Bonnie Henry (British Columbia's Chief Medical Officer) to be honest, kind, sensible, and responsible in their updates and advice. Both provinces have done a good job 'flattening the curve.' As the Peace Country is uniquely physically positioned, I took encouragement from Dr. Henry on May 7, when she was asked about Mother's Day: "Would it be okay to give your mom a hug?" She had such a compassionate look as she addressed the woman on the phone:

We know we are missing our loved ones. I don't want to tell you, you can't hug your mom, but please be wise. Now is the time to double our bubble. But remember, that bubble must still remain small," she cautioned. Later that day Dr. Hinshaw echoed something similar. "I'm not telling grandparents they can't see their grandchildren. I'm asking you to use common sense. I'm trusting Albertans to keep following health guidelines.

What lightness of heart. I was excited to plan a simple walk with my daughter and grandsons. My plan was to be careful, try not to hug them. It's safer to be outside, with one toddler in the stroller and the other little boy distracted by nature, cars, and street noise. I realized early on we weren't going to be able to stay two metres apart. Missing one another's company, my daughter and I kept listing toward one another as we walked. Occasionally my three-year-old grandson would need to be steered back onto the path. My heart melted about halfway through our walk when he asked

"Grandma, can I hold your hand?" Two months without contact. That tiny little touch, his hand in mine, grounded me as nothing else could. It was wonderful and led to more beautiful moments with my family. Visits inside our homes followed—hugs but not kisses, holding and feeding the baby, being close with my daughter. We enjoyed these simple moments, such as my grandsons helping plant flowers and the baby eating dirt and ending up in my tub! So normal. I thought, "I will try to be careful. Not go see them too often."

I went often, until my sore throat came back. I phoned Health Link and a day later was tested for COVID-19. Three days later the test came back negative. The month of May has brought lovely showers of blessings: time with my family; a meal and a visit with my son! Three surprise flower deliveries! The first, from Mrs. Quinn, flowers from her garden. She is dear and thoughtful. The second was from my friend Pauline. We haven't seen each other in person for well over two months.

Pauline looked well, happy to see me and pleased with her surprise gift. My spirit responded in joy. It was so encouraging to see her beaming smile. We live in a strange, but oddly beautiful time, when the presence of a loved one engulfs us so completely that the act of kindness remains rooted in our heart, enabling us to be braver, freer, lighter, grateful, and expectant.

A week later two more flowerpots arrived unannounced. I knew instantly who my benefactor was. My friend Kendra! She has such a kind and generous heart. Again, my heart swelled. Truly I am blessed with many loving friendships.

I was blessed by a visit on my deck with Mrs. Troyer. She has found being at home challenging, and she too has had to be mindful of not getting caught feeling left out of school happenings. The day after our last day at work, the staff had an ice-cream party. Now, though we understood this was coincidental, it still caused a moment of painful response.

"I have to keep myself on a short leash. Not let my brain think too far ahead. If this new life is going to be slower; I need to go with it. Not rush through anything. Take my time and enjoy drinking coffee on my deck." Cheri misses seeing everyone and having a daily routine with purpose. Unemployment insurance pays only half of her salary. This seems unfair. She has found work for June and is hoping to be back at school in September.

Inspired by her daughter Jenna's concern for me, Mrs. Quinn generously dropped off two bags of groceries. It was sweet. Jenna had been listening to the news that encouraged people to look out for those who live alone. I agreed to the delivery, ordered a few things, and planned to pay for my groceries; instead, there were extra treats, and Stacy wouldn't take any money! She has also been feeling blue, restless, discounted, and ruffled. She voiced the same reaction I had to the email announcement of the new EA who was taking over support for both Grade 3 and Grade 4.

She joked, her facial expression oppositional defiance: "I don't want to meet the new EA!" Stacy was kidding. It isn't the new EA's fault (who we have now met and is very lovely); still, our feathers were ruffled. I love this about Stacy, how honest and okay she is with her feelings. Her initial response was natural. Maturity allowed her to recognize that feelings don't always represent the facts, nor are they in charge of our behaviour. COVID-19 is the only reason we don't have job security.

It was a lovely visit with Mrs. Thomson inside my home. Outside of my children, she was the first to enter my home since restrictions were eased. We were careful to stay a safe distance away. She touched as little as possible. Lorraine's face lit up as she walked in. She scanned the room and looked at my pictures. "This is gorgeous...," she marvelled. Lorraine is having a hard time at work. She enjoys all of the staff, but she is missing the kids and bothered by the questions: Will we all work together again? What will school look like in September? What if our job is monitoring hand washing all day long!? It may be a necessary job. How will we separate the children who insist on being in someone else's space? How do we build relationships or teach concepts from six feet away? How do we keep ourselves safe? What if I get a different job? One that pays better and gives me more hours—and if another outbreak occurs, I won't be laid off from? There are a lot of 'What ifs?'

She sighed, "I don't want things to change." None of us do. We recognize that our working environment truly was genuine and supportive and can't be replaced.

The evening before, I sat on my friend Kendra's deck enjoying the sun and companionship. Though she has been by several times with grocery deliveries, we had yet to relax for a longer, less restricted visit. My friends are tired of social distancing. They are careful with hand hygiene and bleach everything inside their house, and now aren't that concerned with how close they get to people outside. I am also a bit less careful. It's strange, this world we now live in. Safe, but... is now the time to engage more socially as there are so few local cases? To enjoy normal activities and spend more time with family and friends? To keep physically distanced, but not be quite as paranoid about it? What's the right thing to do? COVID isn't likely going to kill me, or most people I know. But... there are people who are vulnerable. I have friends I am concerned for and sometimes scared for. I'm not willing to take that risk. It may be that I won't be able to see some friends close up, for months. I try not to think about that.

A few weeks ago, Mrs. V. asked, if we kept two metres away, would I like to go for a walk? Not yet, it's hard to physically distance while walking. The natural inclination is to move toward one another. As for her job, she remains teaching in Grade 5. She continues to learn new ways to engage her students and encourage herself in the process. Hard to believe, but the COVID crisis is hugely overshadowed by the health of one of her students who celebrated his eleventh birthday yesterday. The school had a few gifts for him and his sisters. What a touching moment that must have been for all who participated. His challenges are massive. Chemotherapy once a week for seventeen months... he is just a little boy. Ms. Mergaert has one chemo treatment left, then radiation will follow after she's had time to recover. She seems to be keeping in good spirits, and thankfully the treatments do not cause much nausea. Her two sisters are taking turns staying with her during the week of her chemotherapy treatments, cooking, cleaning, and caring.

I had a deck visit with Ms. Stokes. She is nervous about her position—music is often a casualty when cuts are being made.

Mrs. Backlund thinks she may be ready to talk about these chaotic times by the end of June. Her physical health has been endangered because of the stress COVID has put on teaching practices. She believes that isolation was partly responsible for her depression. Everyone else had another person working in the room with them. For a while this wasn't the case for Mrs. Backlund. However, her new EA is wonderful, and I'm grateful Grace now has such a lovely, capable, calm person working alongside her.

Miss Black, what a difficult position she is in. This week, she finds out how many EAs she is allotted. How will she choose? The good news is, whoever is hired back, they will embody the qualities of Avondale. There are so many unknowns as to what the future might look like. All but three of the teachers are returning, though their job descriptions have changed.

This is an unsettling time for everyone, looking ahead to the challenges and uncertainty of what September may bring, while continuing to do our best to 'thrive' in the present. Avondale staff continues to work hard for their students. Though they have been pushed to their limits, they have risen to the challenge. I doubt they always recognize the profound impact they have on the children under their care.

Mrs. Marshall will soon be on maternity leave. Though the reason for her absence is exciting and positive, she will be missed.

Miss Keddy, Miss Pomeroy, and Miss Hoyseth won't be returning. Sadly, I didn't have a chance to say goodbye or good luck. Where will they go? How are they doing? Their job loss isn't a reflection of their work, but an unfortunate reduction of staffing numbers.

June 27 – Miss Kristina Black

A summation of the last three months of Avondale Elementary 2019/2020 school year: exhaustion, relief, accomplishment, gratitude, and a surprise blessing!

"The most accurate word for how I feel is exhausted." The source of Kristina's fatigue? "The overhanging, unknowing certainty of almost everything. Even in the knowing—when life goes back to normal, it won't really be normal. It is wearing. There's an exhaustion that cannot be relieved with a week's worth of sleep." Typically, Miss Black takes July off to replenish her depleted energy: a trip to Vancouver Island to snuggle her nephew and laugh at his antics, a chance to spend quality time with her family. This year, she has to weigh whether this is safe for her and her family. Alberta Education is preparing for in-person learning in the fall, and many question marks remain. If and how? Though Kristina is looking forward to downtime, the reality is, there is no known cure for coronavirus.

Kristina kept things in perspective when lock-down restrictions were lifted and the number of coronavirus cases in Grande Prairie was low. Balance in her life is a necessity. Bike rides with Riley and Wednesday night golf with friends were helpful for her mental and physical well-being. Normally a planner, Kristina realized the only way through was one day or week at a time. Sleep was manageable as long as she didn't think too hard on the 'what ifs?' She chose to value Avondale's accomplishments more than fear its limitations.

In stressful times, it's a tricky feat to be an optimist, an open door, an effective administrator, and a compassionate shoulder to lean on. And yet, Miss Black seemingly does this effortlessly. Though these qualities are inherent in her, it must be taxing to carry so many burdens: students, parents, and staff. Miss Black's approach is one step at a time. Maintain a grateful heart and eyes to see. She counts herself fortunate. Many people have been laid off or had their business hours restricted, whereas she has had a job to go to each day. Coworkers encourage and brighten her day, sharing her determination to succeed in their mission, despite the trials and hardships.

One of the most endearing qualities of Miss Black is the way she interacts with others, especially with students. They love even the most minor encounter with their principal. A large percentage of her normal school day includes interacting and empathizing with students as she encourages and helps them learn how to problem-solve. March through June, though she checked in with students, her primary responsibilities shifted to the parents still drawing from her exceptional relational skills: empathizing, encouraging, and problem-solving—new technology, worried parents, and hungry children, all issues addressed. She is proud of her staff—the task at hand accomplished. Avondale did the best they could despite circumstances.

Typically, at the end of a school year, teachers and students eagerly anticipate the long, hot days of summer. There is an interesting mix of melancholy, excitement, and lightheartedness. The end of a school year signifies change. The spring months are harmonious, with sunnier dispositions prevailing, the character and chemistry of the classroom firmly established. It is hard to say goodbye. We cheer the students for their successes and award their achievements. The school hosts a small graduation celebration for our Grade 6 students. We're proud of our kids. The report cards' pressure is finally over, and we reminisce and celebrate the school year with a staff barbecue.

Not so this year. Still, where there is a will, there is a way. Like virtual learning, there are no protocols or procedures for saying goodbye to students or giving out awards during a pandemic. The staff collaborated and found creative ways to connect with students and their families—a reverse parade on a perfect Alberta June day, 24 C with a tiny cool breeze. Lined along the parking lot fence were brightly coloured signs wishing the students well. Big red hearts and statements professing how much we miss the students. Avondale staff cheered as parents slowly drove past. Occasionally a vehicle stopped so a student could give their teacher a gift and say goodbye. The heartfelt gifts ranged from mugs to cakes to hand-drawn pictures and cards, to Tim's and Starbuck's gift cards. It was a rare and lovely afternoon in which coronavirus took a backseat. The following morning Miss Black, Mrs. LeClerc, and Mrs. V. delivered plaques to deserving students. The first few houses went according to plan: smile and wave; take a few pictures; congratulate the student for working hard in athletics, academics, or displaying exemplary citizenship. A plaque and name engraved on a trophy are awarded to the student from each grade who excelled in all three categories. The last stop was the year's highlight for Miss Black and capped off a most unusual year. The visit refreshed her waning spirit. For the moment, her worried heart, exhausted mind, and the uncertainties of September were replaced by joyful gratitude. The award for a deserving student turned out to be 'thank you' from an appreciative and grateful parent.

Anisa's mom met them at the door with a radiant smile. "Come in, come in," she urged (going inside did not break any COVID protocols at this point). Behind her, Anisa and her three younger siblings waved and beamed, excited to see their teachers. Attired in their Sunday best for the special occasion, they were adorned with dresses and ties. On the table, was a feast: freshly squeezed mango juice, samosas, and the most delicious pistachio cookies Miss Black had ever tasted. These were just a few of the delights. The children were happy to share stories. The teachers were glad to see how well adjusted the children were. The mother was delighted with her children's education and the genuine care and affection her children received at Avondale Elementary. The morning visit was a surprise blessing. To be reminded that though some families are struggling, others are continuing to thrive. Educators are not always appreciated. They don't require gifts or compliments to do their job well. However, there are times when it is affirming—an acknowledgment of extraordinary efforts made on behalf of their students.

Exhaustion tempered by relief— June 27, a milestone completed. Step one: relief, encouraged by generosity. Step two: encouragement, cautioned by uncertainty. Step three: uncertainty, quelled by family, friends, and purpose. Step four—to be determined.

Part Two

August 29

Where and how to begin? My thoughts are many and are sure to stray. For those returning to Avondale this fall, few were left free of care or unburdened over the summer months. Teachers stressed over how they would physically distance the students' desks, aware that there wasn't enough room to follow the two-metre rule. And how to alter their style of teaching? What about group work? Masks? Yes. No. Yes. Constantly the rules are changing.

For example, there was an earlier announcement in the summer for a return to classes in September. According to data from the federal government, from July 7 to 21, Alberta had the highest provincial per-capita rate of active cases, with the "highest percentage of positive tests."

Alberta's rate of hospitalization was "on the rise and second only to Quebec."

At a July 21 press conference, Premier Kenney said that "we should all be very concerned about the recent rise in active COVID-19 cases." He then announced plans for a "near-normal" return to classes in September with no class-size limits or mandatory masks.

How do you teach five-year-olds when play is limited? Please don't make us have to teach in-person and at-home learning at the same time. Thoughts of school and COVID's impact on our daily and future lives were not the only things on our minds during the summer holidays. We have personal lives and responsibilities, such as reunions with family we haven't seen for months, weddings, and funerals.

My mom passed away on August 4. She spent four days in palliative care, and I am grateful I was with her for most of that time and when she died. Many people during this pandemic have died alone or without loved ones by their side. I came from my mother's womb. Her body nurtured and protected mine. I so wished I could have done the same for her.

While recently walking, I ran into a friend. She is lovely to visit with, and she offered her condolences and asked how I was doing. As I recounted a few of the details surrounding my mother's death and burial, I shared a revelation, "This is the most supported I have ever felt during a time of deep loss." In part, I am more open with people.

I have matured. How can others support me if I don't share how I feel or what is happening in my life? It still isn't a natural response to reach out to others, to assume that they want to know or help. I have to be objective and decipher truth from lies. Truth: I am wonderfully loved and cared for.

My week had been painful, at times tender. There was some running, and a beautiful, blubbering phone call. I had been trying so hard to be okay while I visited with a friend, aware of her pain and desire to enjoy each day with gratitude for the people in our lives. With COVID restrictions, not since the moment of my mother's passing had I fully released the tears of my heart. Unexpectedly, my anguish came gushing out. "I'm sorry," I whispered. My friend wasn't sorry I called or overwhelmed by my heartache. She was touched and pained, present, and empathetic—grateful to be a supportive friend in my time of need. This was a big act of care, but no less valuable to my well-being were the many smaller, loving acts of kindness showered on me.

I left Fort St. John around lunchtime. I don't remember my thoughts driving home other than praying for protection as I drove. I declined my children's offer to drive to Fort St. John. What I needed most was home. My children and grandchildren were a balm. We ate pizza and played in the park. A bit later, Stacy texted—she left a package on my doorstep.

The next morning I received flowers and a visit with Cheri.

My friend Susan and I dashed from place to place looking for a dress for my mom to wear, and then she sent home a strawberry shortcake for a snack. I arrived home to find a package with a lovely card and a mug that reminded me to, 'Be still' from my friend Norma. Many offers of "anything I can do" and "I'm sorry for your loss."

The next evening Mrs. V. brought Crooked Creek donuts, grapes, and a book to read. Visits, phone calls, prayers, cards, gifts, food, and flowers followed. Some of the timeliest blessings were simple texts of "how are you?" or "thinking of you." My friend Kendra and her mom stopped by with cards, flowers, and a basket of fruit. My friend Shelley stopped for a few minutes to offer her condolences and gift me with a lovely book. My friend Pauline came bearing banana muffins baked with tender care and echoed Cheri's desire: "I wish I could hug you."

August 29

Alberta confirmed cases: 13,476, and 237 deaths.

Grande Prairie: twenty-four active, fifty-two recovered, and two deaths (county: fifteen active, and twenty-nine recovered.

Canada: 129,673 cases, and 9,113 deaths.

The United States: 5,939,591 cases, and 182,217 deaths.

The world: 24, 812,440 cases, and 838,704 deaths.

The week before the 2020/2021 school year started many question marks remained. Kristina and Jae were understanding and encouraging, and yet there was so much they didn't know. Policies and procedures were evolving and updated daily. The energy was low. We were happy to see each other and looking forward to seeing the children, sad that we couldn't offer more. We wouldn't be able to respond to them in ways they have come to expect, with maskless smiles and open arms. At our staff meeting, we were an attentive and responsible crew, masked and two metres apart. It was all so unreal. As I looked about the room at each of my colleagues, I knew we would manage. This time of uncertainty would lesson as we adjusted and taught ourselves and the children the best practices for the time being.

The first day of school went better than expected. A few weeks ago, while visiting, Cheri and I agreed that though we were both looking forward to seeing staff and students, we were a bit anxious with all the uncertainty. The most troubling thought was that masks wouldn't be mandatory. We already knew, 'physical distancing where possible' meant our classroom sizes would be larger than fifteen, as per AHS recommendations. A day or two before school began, Alberta Education re-evaluated the current situation and mandated mask use for staff and students, Grades 3–6. They strongly suggested mask use for younger children, K–2. Every kindergarten child arrived proudly wearing an individualized mask. Our hearts hurt a little, watching them find their place at a desk. Instead of small tables where four or five children typically would sit side-by-side and share crayons, scissors, stories, and handholding—they were carefully isolated.

Miss Black told me she hadn't realized just how much she had missed the kids. Truly, they melted her heart. Her steps felt heavy in the spring, and now she noticed she was so happy she almost skipped in the hallways. She was reminded of who she is and what she needs—kiddo relationships. Despite the risks, having kids in the school was better than the alternative.

Our schools provide more than just education and stability for children; we provide for moms and dads too. It takes a village to raise a family.

It was challenging to adhere to the health guidelines all the time. In part, the children are small and still in need of so much help. It's difficult to connect or even get them to focus without kneeling beside their desk. Kindergarten kids are still learning how to work zippers and find stuff in their overcrowded desks. We automatically did things we were advised not to do. The realization came seconds after—we had once again touched something we shouldn't have. The kids were constantly too close to one another. We forgot and sang songs. When we remembered, we sang quieter. How do you teach kindergarten without silliness and movement?

Our kindergarten teacher, Miss Jess, found ways to think outside the box. In time, a vacant classroom provided a space for them to enjoy learning through play. At first, we walked groups of kindergarten children to the washroom and supervised their hand washing. Little ones are so affectionate. They love to hold hands and to give their teachers hugs. How to navigate legitimate needs and behaviours? The same was true of the older children.

It didn't take many days before the smaller children discarded their masks. They took no care as to whether masks were on the floor or covered in cookie crumbs.

We did our best to supervise and remind ourselves and the children of COVID-19 protocols. I found, to my surprise, I wasn't overly anxious or leery of contracting the coronavirus. COVID cases were low in Grande Prairie, and we now knew younger children were less susceptible. I continued to be mindful, washed my hands often, and faithfully wore my mask. I found it was impossible to do my job without coming into closer contact with the students than was advised. Children need undivided attention. When they can't see your whole face, they need to get a good look at your eyes. Do you like me? Are you mad at me? Am I in trouble? Are you happy to see me? Will you help me? It is easy to see how quickly the disease could spread.

The most significant concern for educators was how to catch their students up to grade level. Without question, it's the most pressing problem our children face. Studies show that children who aren't reading at grade level by the end of Grade 3 are unlikely to graduate high school. The responsibility for educators is overwhelming. Concern for their students keeps them awake at night.

In March of 2020, the Alberta Minister of Education announced that all school children would advance to the next grade despite their preparedness. The pressure to perform is unrealistic. We can't discount the five months of missing reading practice. Though technically they are in Grade Two, in hours of learning, they haven't yet finished Grade One!

Each child comes to us with a story. Some parts we know, some parts we don't. We try to prepare and inform without scaring. They have been listening to troubling grown-up conversations. COVID news is everywhere.

It is easy to see and empathize with why we stop listening to the news. It's depressing. And we have lived with the thief in the neighbourhood for far too long. We have stopped listening to others' reports of loss. Our homes are safe. Where we live is free from danger. The thief is sneaky. He doesn't have to steal our possessions to rob us of our peace. It's the threat that he might, that he is more clever, more determined, and persistent to steal than we are to defend.

No matter what position we take (where we stand), whether COVID scared, COVID cautious, COVID cursed, COVID acceptance, or COVID hoax, our bodies, minds, and spirits are bound to be affected. COVID is in control of our thoughts, emotions and feelings. Even balanced thinking requires energy. People have lost freedoms, loved ones, jobs, businesses, opportunities, hopes, special moments, and time with those they love. For those with underlying health issues, they have even more worries to add to their load. They are not overreacting.

In the beginning stages of the pandemic, we were proud as Canadians of our efforts and our governments, despite our ideology leanings.

We banded together in unity, wanting to do the right thing. Each person had their version of what that looked like. We did our best to respect and support one another. I don't envy authorities in power. Their job is thankless, and it's often impossible to make decisions that please everyone. Our county is experiencing division: pro mask; anti-mask. When there is no choice or action that can restore normalcy, we feel powerless. We want answers. We want someone to be responsible. If we can find someone to blame, or we perfectly adhere to the rules, we can go back to normal. COVID doesn't care about normal.

I, for one though, was grateful when our city mandated masks inside public places. It made going for errands and buying groceries a pleasanter experience. I wasn't as concerned about the shopper who wasn't following the arrows or physical distancing requirements. For me, it normalized life. Everyday activities became more enjoyable because I felt protected.

In hindsight, for most of this pandemic, I have probably overreacted to the potential threat. I limited my enjoyment and social gatherings. With the exception of my children and grandchildren, I refrained from close contact with others: a few quick, joyful 'I missed you' hugs, and one shared moment of comfort, despite the pain of the present and the uncertainty of the future. A desire to infuse hope.

At times, I wonder if I followed health guidelines more strictly than some people only because of how I honestly interpreted them. I was, and I am, concerned for our health care system, our elders' health, those who have compromised immune systems, my friends and coworkers, students, family, and myself. Was my careful compliance also an attempt to control or build a layer of protection? Deny a need? Be self-sufficient? Shutdowns are hard on those who tend to isolate when threatened.

November 4

"Busted!" I turned my head towards the sound of the familiar amused voice of Ms. Kay. She was just as out of position, as neither of us was at school this morning. I was searching for pain relief in the drug store. I have fibromyalgia, and I am used to having some aches and pains.

I chalked up my discomfort to the recent loss of my mother and all the uncertainty of COVID and classroom management. This past week my level of pain dramatically increased making it hard to do my job. An x-ray discovered osteoarthritis in my neck and shoulder. My doctor prescribed medication and suggested Tylenol arthritis. (A few weeks later, as the pain worsened, and medications weren't working, the doctor advised a six-week leave. After Christmas break, my hours were lessened to half-time, and my health was evaluated every four weeks in the hope that medications and a variety of therapies would help.)

Jesse and I seldom see each other anymore. I miss our stimulating conversations and shared laughter at the shenanigans of the class, or even just the comfort of quietly working alongside one another. We both look tired because we are. Our spirits pinged at first sight, and the required six feet of distance between us is more like three, even two when we lean in. We reminded ourselves to step back. We were wearing masks, and both of us are careful to follow public health guidelines. We stood face to face visiting for close to twenty minutes. Jessie is used to being able to withstand, roll, and adapt to most challenges. She does so often, with good humour and perspective. We all have limits, and she confessed, one of hers was yesterday. Not one thing in particular, but many stressors on top of one another. School staffers have been in a crisis-teaching mode for eight months now. For Jessie, constant headaches to the point of vision impairment are a definite sign for self-care.

November 22

Cases: Grande Prairie, eighty-six; County, forty-two; total, 128; deaths, four

Cases: Alberta, 46,872; deaths, 471

Cases: Canada, 331,000; deaths, 11,455

Cases: United States, 12.3 million; deaths, 257,000

Cases: Global, 58,275,385; deaths, 1,390,343

November 23

Yesterday, Alberta had the highest number of new cases in the country: 1,584. In the spring and mid-summer, we were proud of how well we were managing. Where once we led the nation in our response, now we are trailing behind. Some people are alarmed, concerned with what lies ahead. The province assures us that there won't be another lockdown. Some wonder, should there be more restrictions? Others deny and live as though COVID isn't much of a threat. They know people who contracted the disease and were hardly affected. To them, financial harm and restricted lifestyles pose a more considerable risk. Some adhere to conspiracy theories created by the government to control us. COVID is no worse than the flu. Fatality numbers are inflated to scare us. Our rights are infringed upon by public health measures that mandate masks and the size of social gatherings.

November 26

The Alberta Government finally imposed stricter measures to combat the out-of-control pandemic. The situation was so bad the contact tracers weren't able to properly do their jobs. Close to three thousand cases had to be abandoned to focus on the most recent ones. Many cases appear to be community spread.

As I listened to Premier Kenny, I heard the heavy in his heart. The weight of many livelihoods rest on his shoulders. Whatever failings he may have made throughout the pandemic, I believe he wasn't discounting the impact coronavirus has had on people. He shared some of the phone calls and emails he received.

There was a phone call from a devastated wife whose husband committed suicide. Between the uncertainty, isolation, and pressures, it seemed too great to bear. Her husband is tragically one of many who have fallen under the spell of 'no way out.' Another call was from a businesswoman with a family-owned business. Their hopes and dreams were slipping away as they struggled to stay afloat. Parents don't have money for food on the table or to pay the mortgage or make rent payments.

Young people, excited to make their mark on the world, have to postpone or cancel plans.

Alberta, the land of opportunity, was losing its glow and cock-sure stance. The province that was rich in resources was struggling even before the pandemic hit. What happened to the idealistic lifestyle we were promised? Though Alberta has a long history of being prosperous for a vast percentage of its population, it isn't an equal playing field for everyone. Working at a school, I see firsthand the imperfections of systems. I also see our business community's generosity and Grande Prairians reaching out to their neighbours and those less fortunate.

Doctor Bonnie Henry highlighted, once again, another major health epidemic: deaths from drug overdoses. The number of people who have died in this manner is staggering. Like COVID-19 patients, most have suffered and died alone. Doctor Henry always reminds us to stay safe, calm, and kind. Compassion is the only way forward. Attacking others' beliefs, attitudes, or actions doesn't produce change.

December 4

I listened to Dr. Hinshaw's medical update, and one reporter's thoughtful question moved me. She asked Dr. Hinshaw how she was doing. Her question acknowledged the mental-health crisis COVID-19 has exasperated. Dr. Hinshaw has urged people to reach out to others in need or for support. Dr. Hinshaw is very calm, and in all her addresses she is wise, thoughtful, polite, and compassionate. This reporter touched her heart. Dr. Hinshaw's face softened, and it took a few seconds for her to regain her sure, even-keeled composure. It was a heartwarming moment that indeed demonstrated and exemplified the notion that 'we are all in this together.' Dr. Hinshaw first thanked the reporter and then replied that she was fortunate to have a loving and sound support system in her family and friends and a close, competent team of coworkers.

Alberta's cases continue to skyrocket. The charts show a sensible, responsible attitude and respect for the virus from March through October. November's response is beyond discouraging. More and more, as people grew tired, with days getting shorter and colder, the denial of coronavirus as a real threat shows up in November's spike. Instead of a gradual, manageable incline, it is vertical and threatens to bring down our health care system. Surveys reveal most Albertans and most Canadians wanted tighter restrictions sooner.

Vaccinations

Good news. The Moderna and Pfizer Vaccine trials are ninety-five percent effective. The optimist in me rejoices in hope. The pessimist in me, or perhaps the realist, cautions celebrating. The process is unknown as of yet. People will need two doses, three to four weeks apart. They are hoping to have all Albertans vaccinated by the end of September. My brain shouts, "We have to live this way for another year!" Though the news is positive, it's also depressing, another reminder of how far we've yet to go. There's confusion and non-compliance with the simple things each of us can do. We want our summer back. Case counts were extremely low, and the outside was safe and enjoyable. We felt much less restricted. We didn't abandon caution but used our judgement to make informed choices. We don't want this!

December 8

Even tighter restrictions were imposed in Alberta. Mandatory masks province-wide were effective immediately. Alberta was the last province to adopt this safety measure. The Premier has been reluctant to do so. Under the circumstances, I don't understand his thinking. And yet, I see, too, my own biased points of view. There is no easy answer to what the world is experiencing. We each have our less-than-perfect response to the continuous cloud that shrouds everything in our lives in a mist of uncertainty. Even the most light-hearted have to work harder to deny that the world we live in is more dangerous than it was. It imposes upon our beliefs. It exposes our differences, challenging marriages, families, friendships and civility. Public Health measures impede our freedom. Social media rushes to enlighten all who are less astute, naïve, or principled than they. Some hide. Some turn every information source off, and continue about their day, unhindered.

There simply seems to be no way to disengage from all the noise of 'what's the right path?' My son says,

The vast majority of the population knows very little about infectious disease. We have great scientific minds working on solutions, so our best bet is to listen to the health experts. I'm not worried about catching the virus. I don't know for sure if wearing masks helps protect me or others or not. I don't like having to wear a mask but it seems like it's the kind thing to do. I don't know who is vulnerable or scared or has an older adult they are worried for. I don't have to be sold on the idea of mask-wearing as legit or not. I just have to care enough about others to make a very small sacrifice to ease their minds. It is far better and safer if the experts are wrong about the effectiveness of masks, as opposed to not trying. It seems so simple. The virus cannot survive if it has no host. We know from other countries' success how to limit and contain it.

One of my friends isn't worried about contracting COVID; still, she wants to do her part. She asks, "If others are having to make sacrifices, shouldn't I too?" For her, it is about respect.

December 13

Only essential businesses are to remain open. Retail services can operate at fifteen-percent capacity. All sporting activities (apart from professionals) are cancelled. Libraries, gyms, and other public centres closed. The Canadian/US border is still closed. Authorities urge, and sometimes plead, limit contacts as much as possible. Work from home if possible. Outdoor fitness in groups under ten is permitted. Single people can walk with a friend as long as they physically distance.

Dr. Hinshaw, "We are trying to bend the curve, not the rules." Single people are allowed to have two close contacts inside their homes.

I have come to recognize I need balance: physical risk, versus a fragile, legitimate need to be physically close to those I love. Research shows that physical affection boosts mental, physical, and spiritual well-being. The country and provincial top doctors sympathize with what's been coined 'coronavirus fatigue.' They urge, 'hang in there.' Friends remind me, though cases have risen in Grande Prairie, they are still relatively low. Be responsible, but don't walk in fear. Choose well and be at peace. Listen to the Holy Spirit's guidance. He is the one I know for sure I can trust. When things get hard, I become more compassionate and understanding of those who have had trouble following guidelines. I'm COVID tired too.

I hadn't realized how much stress I was holding inside until Premier Kenny announced that two single people were permitted to gather at another's household for one Christmas event. I wept with relief and gratitude. My family was perfectly legal to be together on Christmas. It is bizarre to write this. I was torn as to what to do. What was right?

January – March 13

Our kiddos came back to school unregulated, noisy and boisterous. A hybrid extra week of Christmas Vacation delayed their return by a week. School staff returned to schools on January 4, to teach online learning for a week.

Avondale has yet to record a single COVID-19 case. Other schools in our city have had outbreaks and in-person learning suspended. COVID cases Alberta-wide have decreased, whereas our city's cases continue to hover around two hundred. The new strains of the coronavirus variant have yet to impose themselves upon school children. For now, we hold our breath, continuing to prevent, limit, and contain. Student and staff safety is Miss Black's most essential self-proclaimed priority. Fostering and maintaining a physically and emotionally safe environment for Avondale to work and learn is crucial to the school's continued success.

Recently Miss Black listened to Jody Carrington speak. She was shocked to learn the divorce rate in Alberta is up 110 percent! Jody's talk—a snapshot of what our community is experiencing. This is one of the most troubling realities for Kristina. We don't know the sum of the harm our children endure. Crisis is everywhere. There's friction and tension, whether it be open or hidden. As adults, we are often unable to name the emotion we are experiencing. How do we expect children to know why they are wiggly, loud, moody, teary, or unfocused? September onward has provided little opportunity for reflection as Administrators and teachers have worked flat-out. Miss Black, like her staff, like most of the world's population, is tired—exhausted. She doesn't know when she won't be. It's like a new parent with a newborn. It feels like you will be sleep-deprived forever.

The safety of outside gatherings has been such a blessing. We don't stress when the kids are too close together or reach out for a quick hug. They practice soccer skills, pretend they are wolves, play cops and robbers, and enjoy the playground apparatus. They have stopped complaining about COVID. Though not long ago, one of our grade two students felt stressed, and she told me, "My blood is through the roof!" Her hand raised to the top of her head. It took a moment to decipher. What she meant was that her blood pressure was through the roof!

As for our staff, we are managing, though some days, barely. We miss each other. There is less laughter in the hallways as we try to keep up with the many demands of the job. Classrooms continue to grow. Needs are high. Faces are weary but not resigned. No matter how tough the day, or how often our educators feel like they are failing their students, they are not. Our efforts make a daily difference. On our worst days as educators, we have little people who love to come to school and who depend on the stability that their classroom brings.

I asked my friend Jenna Quinn to share her thoughts on what it's been like back in school:

School has been in for six months now. I am so grateful of that. But the bad news is, I am not allowed to hug my friends!! We also have to wear *masks* all the time, and I counted we have to sanitize exactly ten times or more. We go outside we have to wait and wait and wait. We are allowed only two people from each class in the boot room. One time I walked to the bathroom at lunch, so the Grade 2 kids were washing their hands (you are only allowed four in the Bathroom) so I almost missed lunch. *But* still, I am glad schools back.

Jenna Quinn — Grade 4

Jenna and I became friends the moment we first met. Even in kindergarten, she showed an avid interest in reading and writing. Jenna is a helpful and encouraging student who looks out for her classmates. She also likes to draw and make cards to give to people. I have a lovely photograph from kindergarten of Jenna and a classmate showing off their artwork. Displayed on a small whiteboard is "Ms. Powell, Jenna, Sophie," and the acronym, "BFFs." Last year, I was pleased to learn Jenna and I would once again work and learn together in Grade 3. This year, our paths seldom cross, but when they do, our hearts smile. She is an engaging student, and I appreciate her thoughtful questions and answers.

I pray for Jenna and her generation to be careful and thoughtful with their voices as they choose love over hate and apathy. May they choose wisely and be active in their community, knowing they belong and their presence matters. Finally, as adults, I pray we teach and model for them, demonstrating the tools they need to succeed: a good education, determination and grit, resilience, and commitment to honesty, kindness, caring, and courage as they embrace others, themselves, and their futures.

In times of crisis, strengths and weaknesses are brought out in all of us. In my moments of weakness, I isolate, give up, and become discouraged and disheartened. Strength shows up in me through creativity, hopefulness, and gratefulness. I desire to think the best and encourage others. I seek balance. I trust in my relationships. I lean into Lord Jesus who is my source of strength, joy and comfort. COVID-19 challenges, uncertainties, and restrictions have made it abundantly clear how powerless I am to control circumstances. The pandemic is an unavoidable reminder that we often don't know what's coming. We are only given one day at a time, and I want to use my day freely loving and enjoying others and myself. I can only live and love this way through the grace of God—through Jesus.

March 11

One year ago today, the WHO declared a global pandemic. Since then, the news media has updated the number of cases, stirred fear in us with facts or possibilities, searched out inspiring stories, and informed our choices and behaviours. At last, life is finally returning to some measure of normalcy. As this past school year has shown, despite hardships, fears, and exhaustion, we are indeed adaptable.

One of our grade six students, Ella, graced our staff with diamond art pictures. Mine shows Avondale colours: a beautiful cherry blossom tree that sparkles in burgundy, white, and golden hues. The trunk is thick and firmly rooted in the ground. The branches grow in many directions and are connected to the tree's base. If a branch should fall, it withers and dies. However, when they stay connected, they bend in the wind, providing shelter on a rainy day, and shade for overheated travellers. Ella's act of love and generosity was touching and heartens my hope for her generation. It speaks to the power of looking forward and becoming hopeful when things look bleak and grey. The way forward is to turn our hearts and thoughts toward, *"… whatever is true, whatever is honourable, whatever is just, whatever is pure, whatever is lovely… think about these things"* (Philippians 4:8, ESV).

This is where we are March 11, 2021, one year later. Each story has only just begun, twisting and turning, with steep hills and low valleys, green grass, and hard, desolate ground. Sometimes the landscape appears vast, open, and teaming with exciting possibilities. Our steps are taken in tandem. There's a dream to share; a hand to hold, secure and familiar. Other times, the path appears narrow, lonely and dangerous, and every movement requires painstaking deliberateness. Every day, we begin again: taking one small step after another. Whether physically apart or together, we are fortunate to have fellow travellers with whom to traverse and share this life. Where our stories take us, I do not know—for now, I wait to take my next small step.

March 13, 2021

Grande Prairie cases:1,583; active, 204; deaths, twenty-three
Alberta cases:137,364; deaths, 1,938
Canada cases: 903,022; deaths, 22,401
World cases: 119,113,952; deaths, 2,641,743

Part Three

July 15

My next small step took place as a result of receiving a Braun Book longlist award for our Journal entry. It was Kristina who most urged me forward. Immediately, she offered ways to raise money so I could publish. Her enthusiasm and confidence bubbled over, and soon I felt inspired to write a Part Three to update the remainder of the 2020/2021 school season, March 12–June 28, 2021. The end date coincided with Alberta lifting its COVID-19 public-health restrictions on July 1, 2021.

After I finished my manuscript, I lost the energy and urgency to continue recording my thoughts and opinions. I grew tired of talking about COVID-19 and noticed how seamlessly I could slip into places of fear and negativity. Undoubtedly, the last year and a half have been fraught with challenges. Some have been met with success, appreciated, and gleaned from, while others are a work in progress.

My thoughts were scattered, and unfocused as negative emotions kept me off balance. Sometimes subtle, and other times overtly demanding. I was tempted into silence by both optimism and cynicism as the two sharply contrasted my moods. My sincere desire was to be encouraging and transparent in my sharing, and yet I obsessed over whether I could let myself be seen as I am—my sentiments of a hopeful and faith-led woman, with tears and cluttered, less than ordered and optimistic thoughts. As I reflected, I realized both expressions are genuine. I'm valid and valued. My experiences matter to God, others, and myself.

The legitimate threat of an unknown virus, along with COVID-19 public restrictions, triggered an old way of thinking: don't need, don't ask. Make myself and my problems small. The old way is uncomfortable and ill-fitting. The pandemic was, and is, not a small problem. We need others, always. It is the loving way to admit to, ask for, and allow others to meet our needs. Love is meant to be reciprocal, and when it is, as trust grows, we start believing our needs are valid and will be met by trusted people.

For the last six weeks, my body and brain have felt sluggish as I trudge through a low, dry, parched valley. I have days where my steps are firmer and my countenance lighter. I admire the greenery and enjoy the vivid, colourful flowers that grace my surroundings. My heart is grateful and tender, and handled with care. It takes persistent effort to keep pushing forward. My Bible encourages me, *"give thanks in all circumstances..."* (1 Thessalonians 5:18, ESV) and, *"... press on toward the goal for the prize of the upward call of God in Christ Jesus"* (Philippians 3:14, ESV).

Press on, upward, towards. Complete the task. Focus on my original intended goals:

1. Record history.
2. Update the conclusion of Avondale Elementary 2021 school season.
3. Share my struggles.

1. History

Though my journal originally ended on March 11, 2021, the pandemic did not.

Cases in Canada, Alberta, and Grande Prairie continued to rise through the spring, as did the concerns of most of the public health officials and professionals.

On May 1, 2021, Premier Kenny announced tighter restrictions, including schools going back to At-Home Learning for the week following Spring Break. The measures the province imposed were the most extreme since the beginning of the pandemic and heightened the already existing discord between the most passionate of the two opposing beliefs. Too little too late, versus freedom of rights and opposition to the government.

Alberta experienced several days of record-breaking daily case numbers and over 20,000 active cases. Test positivity—around ten percent. Grande Prairie and its surrounding county hovered around seven hundred active cases.

Alberta entered stage two of their reopening plan on June 10, 2021, two weeks after sixty percent of the eligible population had received at least one vaccine dose, and hospitalizations for COVID were below five hundred. This milestone meant people could gather in groups of twenty outdoors while still practicing physical distancing. Social gatherings indoors weren't allowed. Places of worship, entertainment, recreational facilities and retail could open at one-third fire-code capacity. Wedding and funeral services permitted twenty people, both inside and outside, but larger receptions could be outdoors. Personal and wellness services could resume walk-in appointments. Indoor dining was once again allowed after many months of take-out and was no longer restricted to the same household. Youth and adult sports resumed both indoor and outdoor without restrictions. Public outdoor gatherings could include as many as 150 people. Fixed grandstands could reopen with one-third capacity. The work from home order was lifted but recommended where possible. Distancing and masking requirements remained in place.

Health Canada approved three vaccines: Pfizer, Moderna, and AstraZeneca.

Skeptics worried about the safety of vaccines because of how quickly they were developed. However, scientists explained that the historical blueprint used for years for coronaviruses was followed, and no health regulation steps were skipped.

The vaccine distribution was prioritized in each province according to the most vulnerable populations. Thus, the elderly, frontline workers, and the immune-compromised were selected as the first recipients. After these groups received their doses, availability opened up according to the year a person was born, working from oldest to youngest.

The combination of vaccinations, restrictions, and time of year seemed to result in a heartening plunge in the number of active cases in our city, province, and country.

On July 1, 2021, Alberta entered Stage 3 of the Open for Summer Plan. (Recently, a friend pointed out the addition of, 'for summer' as a subtle reminder that health officials and the governments are cautious about the potential for cases to rise in the fall.) All public health measures were lifted, except for isolation and quarantine requirements and some healthcare settings and public-transit restrictions.

Hoping to boost and ensure most of the population chose to receive the vaccine, the province sponsored a vaccine incentive—Open for Summer Lottery—three chances at a million dollars for those who had both doses. The contest included smaller prizes such as tickets to the Calgary Stampede. As well, there was the Outdoor Adventure Vaccine Lottery for a chance to win hunting, fishing, or camping experiences. The WHO accused richer countries, including Canada, of hoarding vaccines, warning that until the vast majority of the world was vaccinated, COVID-19 would continue to be a severe health threat. The new emerging Delta variant was a considerable concern, and experts warned the world was in a race to vaccinate the most people possible to combat its threat. Canada donated 17.7 million vaccine doses of AstraZeneca to the COVAX, sharing initiative.

The following entries, July 28–30 came as a surprise and were written after my journal was completed. I felt it was important to include these additions.

On July 28, Alberta was the first province (and at that time only province) to announce a new COVID-19 policy. The Health Minister said, "We are leading the way in moving to the endemic (phase of the COVID-19) response. We have led the way throughout in the response to the pandemic, quite frankly."

Starting July 29, there would be no more mandatory masking, contact tracing, or isolating, and by August 16 (this time was later extended by six weeks due to rising case numbers), isolation following a positive test would no longer be required but strongly recommended. Their decision caught everyone off guard—Alberta COVID cases were rising once again, and we had one of the highest rates of unvaccinated people in the country and the lowest rate of first doses. The provincial government's decision to remove public-health protocols was part of preparing for other diseases in the fall. The percentage of the population vaccinated had decreased the coronavirus risk to the healthcare system and the general population—stating it was now time to treat COVID-19 as any other respiratory disease.

July 30, early on in the pandemic, we learned the term R-value: effective reproduction number. It is a way of measuring an infectious disease's capacity to spread. It represents the number of people who will become infected by one person. Alberta's R-value was at one of its highest rates, though daily case numbers were pretty low (CTV News).

As expected, this news garnered much attention. Critics claimed Alberta's actions were reckless and irresponsible. Those in agreement thought restrictions should have been lifted sooner or not imposed in the first place. Others cheered and celebrated, and some were both hopeful and a bit skeptical.

The common denominators throughout the pandemic were the propensity for opinions to take precedence over people, and the struggle to determine what was true. Even when, or if, we trusted in facts, we still couldn't negate suffering. Instead of acceptance and empathy, we chose to voice our displeasure through blame, furthering the gap between those who don't live or think as we do. I am right, and you are stupid. I am ambitious, and you are lazy. I am strong, and you are weak. I am generous and open-minded, and you are cold and selfish. I am kind, and you are not. Fear, exhaustion, confusion, apathy, and entitlement can lead us to view our opinions as more than what they are: a judgement or belief not necessarily based on fact or knowledge.

2 Avondale Elementary

On March 12, Avondale joined the list of schools with its first confirmed COVID-19 case. Staff members scrambled to implement protocols with a flurry of phone calls to parents and work to be sent home. The protocols held, and our confidence and comfort level grew. Cohorts and warmer weather afforded opportunities for kids to be closer to one another with less risk. We wondered though, would one case lead to an outbreak? We welcomed our little and big friends into the building two weeks later, happy and reassured to see no outbreak or severe illness. We added two more cases in April. Fortunately, they coincided with Easter Break, so apart from our concern for those infected, the mood of our school wasn't affected.

May was met with tired gratitude. We had weathered the worst of the COVID storm, and the growing population of those vaccinated eased some concerns. I don't recall anyone overly stressing about the possibility of another school closure, as the numbers were climbing; we knew it was a possibility. The news and situation in India were truly frightening. Could the vaccines stand up to the mutating virus? Would enough people choose to receive the vaccine so we could reach herd immunity and protect those with compromised immune systems and our younger children? Our student population is under the age of twelve, and though a worrisome possibility, for now, we pushed aside the threat of new, more contagious variants. Staff members didn't have enough energy to fret about one more thing. Efforts to be cheerful and engaging, checking in with the students and with one another sustained and motivated our resolve. The urgency to prepare the students for the next grade weighed heavily on everyone. As did the security of job placement with Avondale come September.

In June, two more cases and two classrooms were sent home to isolate. As a small, close-knit group, the absence of so many students and staff dampened spirits further. June is usually a robust and happy time. We didn't want 2021 to end the way 2020 had—without a chance to say goodbye to our students. Thankfully, our entire school finished the last four days of school. Sunshine cooperated as classrooms enjoyed field trips to nearby parks and an organized outside play day. Several days of frozen treats lifted the spirits of hot and thirsty participants.

On the last day of school, eight-year-old Nina approached me at lunchtime. She wanted to tell me that she wasn't going to cry today. I smiled. The past two Fridays, she had drawn close and rested her head against me. When I reached down to look into her face, her eyes glistened with tears. Concerned, I asked, "What's wrong?" "I'm going to miss you," she gulped. Both times I assured her summer holidays were weeks away.

The last day was filled with fun until the final few moments of the day. The little girl who sat behind Nina was unusually solemn. "I'm sad. I don't want school to be over." I felt a tug at my heart. "It's okay to be sad. I'm sad too." I glanced at Nina. Her resolve not to cry was crumbling. "Nina is sad too. Even though it is exciting to finish Grade 2, it's still hard to leave our friends for the summer. We can be sad and excited at the same time. And I will still be here next year." I promised. With that, their attention seemed to shift. Kid-friendly chaos ensued as Miss Stokes presented each student with a year-end gift bag from the two of us. Minutes later, the classrooms and hallways were empty and quiet.

The district school calendar allotted an extra day for staff members to clean up their spaces and help out with general year-end cleaning, organizing, and sorting. Though there is always plenty of physical work in need of doing, the day was relaxed and casual. It allowed for quieter, reflective moments between individuals and small clusters of staff—a luncheon hosted by administration (Miss Black/Mrs. Leclerc) held in the gymnasium highlighted our school's genuine affection for one another as we cheered successes and wished those who wouldn't returning well. We respected public guidelines as we physically distanced and listened to Miss Black's heartfelt address. "I can honestly say this is the most trying year I have ever experienced." Mrs. Leclerc presented beautiful handmade chartreuse trays her husband had crafted for staff who wouldn't be returning next year. When Mrs. Quinn received her gift, Kristina readily assured us that she was sure a position would open up in September for Mrs. Quinn. I sure hope so. She is a wonderful EA, friend, and coworker. The most delicious, luxurious cheese, crackers, meat and fruit boxes felt fitting for the occasion: the finest for the finest, a banquet to celebrate the esteemed guests of honour—our Avondale staff. We are stronger, more empathetic, and more appreciative of the significance of the work that we do. We can be proud of our accomplishments and the knowledge that we make a difference in the lives of children and those we work with.

What is hopeful and encouraging about this year's summer vacation is the promise of a well-deserved and much-needed rest for educators everywhere. For all the difficulties and uncertainties, Avondale as a whole met the unwanted gift of adversity—the 2020/21 coronavirus pandemic.

Many months ago, we determined that we would teach and model resiliency. We set out to pioneer a new way, a hard way. It was satisfying and rewarding as we worked together and relied on each other for hope, encouragement, levity, resources, and direction. Leadership set priorities and led by example. Our heart mission remained the same— keep showing up and determine how we can best serve our students and their families.

With appreciation and a more settled state of how schools can operate during stressful and unknown circumstances, teachers can rest and enjoy their summer vacation this year. Miss Black/Kristina is planning a trip to Vancouver Island to visit and hug her family and laugh with delight over her two-year-old nephew.

Stacy's postponed trip to Vancouver Island was realized as she and her family returned home last night. It was everything they had hoped for.

Mrs. Troyer and her family spent a beautiful week at Banff National Park.

Miss Stokes was adventurous and went camping with friends.

Several staff members have plans to spend part of the summer on the east coast with family and friends they haven't seen in two years. Hot, lazy days in the sun with a good book, dips in the pool, and outings with friends and families are sure to revive spirits. A sense of excitement will once again return in September.

3. Me

From March to the end of May, I felt like I was solid and grounded. I went to work each day feeling capable and with a smile on my face. So, I was unprepared as I stepped off the page of May and tumbled into June.

The bruises, cuts and scrapes I incurred didn't appear deep or in need of careful attention. Nothing was broken, and yet, the climb loomed large. My legs felt weak, and my mind was unfocused and misty.

June 1

Today was my mom's birthday. She would have turned eighty-seven. When I arrived at school this afternoon, I learned the sad news that Jae's mom had passed away. I am grateful she and her mom had several months of enjoying and loving one another before it was time to say goodbye. Losing a loved one is very painful, even when you know the certainty of the outcome, as I experienced in my mom's passing this past year.

June 4 – Staff professional learning day

My health was poor. I was vulnerable, sad, lonely, and tired, which made it difficult for me to feel peaceful. As I sat and listened to my friends and colleagues progress over Teams, I admired and acknowledged each of their genuine commitments to our students. We are a wonderful group of Educational Assistants who are compassionate and competent professionals and human beings. The thought of some of us not working together next year felt sad.

June 5

"How are you?" A friend asked through a text.

From the book, I'm reading, "Those roundabout ways we take are paved with stones God himself lays. God cares about you. Your situation is not a litmus test to prove God loves you. If you feel you are in the middle of nowhere, it doesn't mean you are. You are climbing higher and higher in God's purpose" (Grace in the Valley by Heath Adamson).[1]

Low, slow,
No glow, no flow,
Today I choose to row,
To grow,
To trust not in what I feel,
But in what I know.

I am not in the habit of responding to texts by rhyming, and yet the words described how I felt, as had the word, 'nowhere.' The quote reminded me that what I see and feel doesn't always align with the truth and God's perspective, his care and purpose for my life. When life is hard, the future uncertain, and my emotions and body are passing through moments of pain, the way forward is to grasp the hand of my Father. Believe he is who he says he is, and I am who he says I am: "... *fearfully and wonderfully made*" (Psalm 139:14a, ESV).

---

[1] Heath Adamson, *Grace in the Valley.* (Baker Publishing Group, Grand Rapids, MI, 2018), 105.

June 6

A busy, active afternoon with my grandsons restored my sense of stability. We laughed. We hugged and squeezed. We played. And I chased. I am so grateful that they live close by, and I can spend time with them. When I am with them, I know exactly who I am to them—Grandma.

June 7

I found out today that I have a position in September, for which I am thankful.

June 10

COVID symptoms kept me home from work. Doctors discovered an alarming trend they called Long Haulers. It describes some coronavirus patients as suffering long-term effects from the disease. I don't want to get sick, nor can I afford to be.

June 12

COVID test was negative.

June 13

This morning I read, *"A cheerful heart is good medicine, but a broken spirit dries up the bones"* (Proverbs 17:22, NLT). One translation said 'sad heart' as opposed to a 'broken spirit.' I haven't considered seriously that the pandemic—the fears, uncertainties, isolation, loss of physical and social connection, along with my mom's passing, has broken my spirit. And that much of my low state is because I am sad. My cousin Elaine said it is tough to be cheerful or pursue creativity when you are grieving, weary, overwhelmed, and financially stressed. According to the Proverb, the cure for my hurting bones, failing health, and lagging spirits will be a joyful, cheerful heart that returns as I mourn my losses and pass through times of brokenness.

June 14

I received more than a dozen hand-made birthday cards from our Grade 2 class. It was very sweet. Multiple birthday wishes from friends and a phone call from my brother warmed my heart. The evening before, I was grateful and content as I enjoyed dinner and cake with my son, daughter, son-in-law, and two grandsons. Drive-by visits and gift deliveries in the following days cheered my heart.

June 16

A timely and thoughtful text from Cheri asked how I was feeling. I admitted to feeling low, sad, and a bit broken. She offered to call. Her care and my honesty brought a tender and grateful response: tears gathered at the corners of my eyes, and my throat constricted. I considered saying, please, do call, but hesitated and then declined. I was sure to cry at the sound of my friend's voice, and we both needed to be at work soon.

June 17

I felt moved to do something positive for our school's hard-working, tired team. I wondered how I could encourage them. I chose a cheerful or hopeful card to put in their mailboxes.

June 17

I arrived at school in time for outside recess. The big kids were away, so, for a treat, the Grade Ones and Twos had a chance to play on the Grade 3–6 playground. A handful of boys were on the basketball court, and when they spotted me, they called out, "Ms. Powell, come play with us!" The weather was cool that day; the fresh air was helpful for both my head and stomach. Their faces were eagerly awaiting my answer. How could I refuse them? I've been cautious since I fell last fall and was diagnosed with osteoarthritis. I would be careful, and without many weeks left of school, I wanted to have fun with them. Besides, I enjoy playing with them and appreciate their efforts and skills. All was well until one of their feet tripped me up.

It was such a shock when my body hit the ground. After I stood up, my stomach lurched, and I felt faint. I found a bench and tried to gather myself as I stripped off my coat. My head swam in circles, and my knee and hands stung. Miss Elliott sent me home, promising she would help out with my job. Later, I was surprised by how jarring my fall was to my well-being. It was another reminder that I wasn't okay. A year ago, I likely wouldn't have tripped. My legs and balance would have prevented the fall. What would I do if I couldn't work at this job?

June 18

Due to my fall the day before and the residual side-effects from my vaccine shot, I cancelled a walk with a friend. I felt unwell and slightly defeated. My heart was sad and disappointed. Though we texted and talked often, we hadn't visited each other in person for a long time. So, I was surprised when my friend texted to say she was outside my door with a birthday present and a heartwarming smile.

We made plans to have a telephone visit the next day.

I shared that something I read led me to count how I have experienced loss throughout the last year and a half of the pandemic. Sharing helped me process my experiences. My losses included job earnings, the loss of physical comfort, security and joy of shared embraces, and a sense of loss of connectedness from spending so much time alone. Not long before the lockdown, I discovered a game called pickleball that I really enjoyed. It was fast, required agility, quick hands and feet, and engaged my mind. I loved it. Now, even walking sometimes hurts my shoulder.

The conversation with my friend bolstered my confidence and validated my feelings, prompting me to make a necessary phone call. An hour later, I called her back with good news! I shared the update with other friends as well. It was a huge relief.

Earlier that morning I read, *"Jesus saw the huge crowd... and he had compassion on them"* (Mark 6:34, NLT). Jesus looks after the widows, and he looks after me.

June 21

With just over a week before provincial COVID-19 restrictions are lifted, it seems most people are already enjoying and embracing the freedoms of normal life. However, I am still struggling to feel my well-self. I want to feel happy and content.

When asked how I am doing, sometimes I answer, "not all that well," or, "just okay."

It is difficult for my friends and family to know and understand the extent of my struggle, as, at times, my answers are evasive and downplay my feelings, circumstances, and experiences. The act of slipping on a mask seems second nature. In some moments I'm not able to admit to what is painful and unpleasant. I wonder, as I express this thought, if the person I hide most from is me?

Forced isolation and minimal social interactions have been challenging for those of us who live alone, have flawed coping skills, and tend to think deeply about things. I recognize my thinking is off-key, and I know I am richly blessed and have a good life. The hole I am stuck in isn't overly dark, nor life-threatening. It is more like the ground is rife with potholes that hamper the ease of my walk. Or I find myself in a sand trap, and it takes several swings to get myself out of the hazard. Yet, when I am with my family, friends, or community, the unease lessens, and my laughter, care, and interest are genuine. I am okay and in the moment. It is unsettling. My brightness and surety are bullied by pessimism. The banter between the two is exhausting. I need people.

June 29

I asked Miss Stokes if she would save a book for me from Mr. Buziak's collection. She chose a book from the '60s on spirituality. While I don't agree with everything, one part was significant—another reminder of some wisdom a friend and I have discussed.

Of late, it feels like I am having continuous reactions to my reactions. When I react, I judge whether my response is negative or positive, and I'm not showing objectivity or unconditional love. Part of our job as educators is to encourage children to learn new ways of responding to challenges. Rather than react impulsively to the challenge, instead, breathe, and wait for the uncomfortable feeling to pass. Make a choice that redirects to achieve calm and curiosity that develops self-confidence and the desire to succeed. We are in the process of learning and appreciating the importance of positively framing words from unhelpful to helpful. When used effectively, this does increase confidence and cooperation. I use my words and gentle spirit every day to encourage others, and I am worthy of the same care and respect from myself.

July 1

Home from an overnight trip to Edmonton with my daughter and four-year-old grandson. This was my first venture anywhere in a long time. The weather was staggeringly hot all week, and Alberta broke record-high temperatures. My former in-laws invited us to an outside supper in their backyard. The shade provided some relief, and our visit was lovely. It was the first real sense of normal I had experienced in ages, and it took me back through the years. Eleven years have passed since I last sat outside on their deck, enjoying a meal and conversation together. I miss the comfort and companionship we shared over the years.

An overnight stay in a hotel allowed simple, ordinary, real-life experiences I haven't enjoyed since before the pandemic. My grandson was excited and sweet as he held my hand and chatted away. Time with my daughter is a treasured gift. I look forward to babysitting her other son tomorrow morning for the day. He is two. Such a cute and busy age!

July 1 (Cases, Recoveries, Deaths, and Vaccinations)

Grande Prairie: 3,960, cases; 3,907 recoveries; twenty-nine deaths; 54.5 percent (one dose); thirty percent (second dose).
County of G.P.: 1,413 cases; 1,406 recoveries; five deaths.
Alberta: 232,000 cases; 229,000 recoveries; 2,307 deaths; 73.1 percent (one dose); 44.8 percent (second dose).

Canada: 1, 420,000 cases; 1,390,000 recoveries; 26,401 deaths; 68.5 percent (one dose); 32.1 percent (second dose).
World: 185,291,530 cases; 4,010,834 deaths.

July 2

My day with my grandson was fun, though tiring. He climbs on and jumps off everything, and "I try" is spoken often with emphasis. He also likes grandma to carry him, which of course I do! We played in the sandbox with dinosaurs, and after a bath, rocked and snuggled with a book.

When I got home, I read my emails.

A flutter of excitement when I read the note from the publisher that my manuscript made the Longlist. And then, a strange occurrence, I didn't know what to do with the news. Of course, those I shared with were happy for me. Kristina's excitement encouraged me to type. Reflection requires honesty and openness to hear your heart and then receive and respond to its insight. Though I felt blessed by the beautiful getaway with my daughter and grandson, and the ease and genuine affection between me and my former in-laws, a sense of tenderness and loss tugged at my heart.

July 3

It's only in the last few months that I am noticing how much I have aged. The effects of the pandemic are evident in every area of my life. I wasn't one of those people who threw themselves into fitness, crafting, or learning a new skill. Instead, my inactivity may have led to increased pain and physical weakness. My body and mind ache and feel listless. I know that I need exercise and physical outlets like golf and pickleball. It is vital for my body, mind, and spirit. I am athletic, creative, and competitive. There is a huge hole in my heart from not engaging in activities that bring me joy.

I haven't physically attended church in close to two years. I have a longing for spiritual connection through prayer and worship with other believers. Isolation from COVID restrictions exposes my deeper insecurities, triggering a false sense that my destiny is to live life primarily alone: don't ask, don't need, as the old ways re-emerge. In recent years, the walls and compartments in and around my heart had mostly dissolved. My faulty thinking had crumbled to the ground, replaced with new, healthy, constructive thinking. The combination of fear, pain, and forced isolation cloud my thinking. I recognize that not all thoughts and feelings are a true reflection of reality. An anxious brain doesn't always reason well.

I struggle to act upon what I know in my heart to be true; the cure for my ailments and insecurities is to reach out to others, to look outward and upward. Go to church, exercise, get involved, volunteer. Take the next step. This always includes being honest with myself and others.

Asking

Just typing the word 'asking' causes my insides to knot.

As I write what I felt, it's tricky to stay present, to not get pulled into the undercurrent of unease that tells me I'm not okay or I've done something wrong.

I wonder if sharing some of my struggles will benefit, add to, or distract from the overall purpose of the journal? Will my openness be an embarrassment, hurt, or cause discomfort for myself or others? I have a voice, feelings, and experiences that sometimes feel big. When I am afraid or discouraged and struggle, I can refuse the bait that tells me I am falling short and missing the mark and that I need to apologize for needing or feeling low and lacking energy.

I am tired, isolated, and feeling both a physical and an emotional ache that it seems won't go away. My affectionate, tender, and empathetic heart hurts for many people experiencing loss and pain through COVID. I feel melancholy. And yet, as my trust is tested and I question my faithfulness and how firmly I am *"... rooted and grounded in love"* (Ephesians 3:17, ESV), Lord, you hear my cry. You hear my heart and lead me in your loving kindness to the rock that is higher, out of the pit, the mud, and the mire of old thoughts and isolating thinking that held me captive—pressed from the hope that you set before me. My tears are held in your hands. The trail is narrow, and past journeys through dark and rugged terrain have taught me this is true. Still, it takes courage to trust that vulnerability can be a friend and not a foe.

Humility and acceptance trickle down my cheeks.

July 6

My friend Pauline has a thoughtful and insightful mind, and her words and expression of speech are beautifully simple, straightforward, and wise. Our conversation today was reflective and interesting. I asked that she text me her thoughts as they captured some of what I believe to be a powerful message. Though unwanted, the adversity of the pandemic has brought the opportunity to build resilience in each of us. It is our responsibility to choose how we respond. Choice is always followed by consequence and often requires a difficult sacrifice as we let go and consciously turn our attention towards pursuing hope.

Some thoughts that come to mind.

Thrive… the life that comes out of choosing to live each day well in every circumstance of life, no matter what comes. During times of adversity, it is especially important that we develop resilience and the hope needed to overcome and become adaptive and grow and connect with others. We must focus on these things:

- Adaptability
- Quick learning
- Creative problem solving
- What we can do instead of what we can't do
- Admitting/acknowledging needs, including emotions/ mental health. Adversity shows us our need to connect with others.
- Not losing heart/purpose though fatigued

- Becoming comfortable with the discomfort of not being in control
- Attitude is our choice

Choose joy rather than fear, whether we feel it or not, because we are examples to little ones. They need to see the grown-ups in their lives as able to contain themselves and thrive.

There is an incredible, positive influence and impact for good in showing up for the children and families in your care as a school family. When you show up with energy, hope, creativity, and a smile in your eyes, you are holding out a light of hope (during COVID) that will continue to ripple out and make a good way forward for the many in your care.

Being brave, having courage in reaching out, and connecting honestly in sharing ourselves with others builds a safe haven and community for others to reach out to us. I see you. I hear you. I care, and I'm here. Every child needs to know this, and it helps them thrive.

Our conversation reminded me of the one Grace (Mrs. Backlund) and I had just over a year ago. We were contemplating the word 'thrive.' At the time, Grace felt overwhelmed, and thriving felt like an unattainable goal, in direct opposition to the distress she was feeling. Even so, her dedication and perseverance didn't allow her to take any shortcuts to the finish line. She kept putting one foot in front of the other. One small step at a time rewarded Grace with a successful year in 2020/21. Last year's struggle to adapt and learn quickly was replaced with a sense of satisfaction as Grace excelled at school and At-Home-Learning. She is an example and inspiration. She demonstrates that if we keep choosing to try, engage, be honest, and see our failures and trials as opportunities to thrive, we will succeed at what matters most—relationships. As adults, the most significant and influential roles and responsibilities we have are to provide safe, nurturing environments where children can grow and thrive. With deep, consistent, patient, gentle, generous and unconditional love, our children will succeed, and so will we.

Despite the low valley I am currently experiencing, I am confident my stay will yield rewards. As I reflect upon this time in history and appreciate how richly I was and am blessed, the strongest and most impactful remembrances from this past eighteen months are joyful, incredibly touching, and tender. I have shared affection, grief, victory, and many simple and 'oh so beautiful' moments of thoughtfulness— from phone calls to five-minute driveway visits; bags of groceries to special deliveries of medicine, and six potatoes for an upset stomach; delight in my grandsons' faces as we squeezed each other tight. A Zoom meeting, a Bible verse, a song, a picture, a laugh, all remind me I am not alone. We are all part of many beautiful, complex, intricate storylines. Our honesty and willingness to engage and connect with God, ourselves, and others water the dry places in our lives. Every exchange and act of kindness is a gift that draws us closer to God and one another.

What I missed most throughout the pandemic was the sharing of warmth, delight, concern, and shared pain in the eyes of family and friends. I missed wrapping my arms around them in joy, just because I was with them. I missed hugs of comfort and shared pain—all exchanges and embraces that speak directly to our hearts: "I love you."

July 27

The goodness of God is always present, but sometimes it is timing that makes all the difference. A sequence of events revived my weary heart.

First, an unexpected gift from my friend Shelley who called to offer her congratulations regarding my manuscript. Our conversation quickly turned to praise for God. We talked. We praised. We prayed. Her call reminded me of the simple but powerful act of thankfulness, mindfully practicing "thank you." Teaching our children to say please and thank you is about more than teaching good manners and respect. It develops a thankful attitude and directs our hearts toward gratitude, joyfulness, and a sense of contentment and belonging. Our visit affirmed that close relationships endure time and physical distancing more effectively when we hear each other's voices. Our visit opened the eyes of my heart to ask and to receive.

Before leaving for my mom's Celebration of Life Gathering, I stopped to see my friend Pauline. The night before, I texted to see if she had time for a quick visit outside. A hug and a moment of prayer allowed me to release a few tears. They slid down my cheeks, gentle and free. In my anxiousness, I was afraid to admit to and ask for a simple act of care and affection. Now, I relaxed and rested in the 'normal' unabashedly needed, joyful, safe, loving hug I had missed and sought out.

The following morning, I enjoyed a lovely visit with my aunt and uncle, who drove up from Saskatchewan for my mom's Gathering. Unfortunately, COVID concerns and restrictions prevented them and many others from attending my mom's graveside service last summer. I'm grateful my aunt and uncle had the chance to visit my mom last March before everything shut down. My uncle shared one of my mom's clearer moments while they were with her. She looked him square in the eye and exclaimed, "Wouldn't it be great if Jesus just came and took me away?!" Then, for emphasis, my mom flung her hand towards heaven.

Though we live in different time zones, and our visits through the years have been few, the smile in my aunt's eyes and her open arms invited me into the same loving, encircling, heart-touching embrace that I had experienced the morning before. I had expected to feel gladness but was surprised by how comfortable and comforted I felt. Through our exchange, we rejoiced and mourned my mom's life and the gift of each other's presence. We share many traits and beliefs. I confided, "This feels like hugging one of my best friends." Her smile broadened, and her voice croaked, "I know, it's like we are kindred spirits." I felt known and accepted, welcomed in a way that spoke to my heart—-safe, cared for, and part of. Moments such as these are what we all long for. All of us seek to be known, heard, loved—accepted, needed, and valued.

My son shared a powerful quote that echoes and clarifies my thoughts on how pandemic opinions and attitudes influenced the level of friction between opposing views. When left unchecked, opinions tend to bulldoze over sensitivity.

Opinion is really the lowest form of human knowledge. It requires no accountability, no understanding. The highest form of knowledge… is empathy, for it requires us to suspend our egos and live in another's world. It requires profound purpose larger than the self kind of understanding. (goodreads.com Bill Bullard)

Though at times opinions may be engaging, humorous, encouraging, and helpful, it wasn't other people's opinions that lifted my spirits or provided a source of comfort and connection. I didn't long for the touch or face of an opinion. My principal, Kristina, wasn't moved to start a Go-Fund-Me campaign because she believed in her opinions. My family, friends, and coworkers' support was born out of love and empathy, and a sense of being part of something bigger than themselves. Empathy and purpose transform lives. It was others' willingness to sit with me in times of sorrow and unrest, as well as their cheerleading in my day-to-day experiences, that made me secure and confident in my heritage—my place of belonging. Avondale Elementary excels at doing the same for both staff and students. The power of empathy is why the Avondale COVID Journal began and the reason for its publication.

I pray I don't substitute my opinions for facts or truth or become so attached to them that I miss the opportunity to understand another as I enter into their world. Instead, I will listen and use my words and actions to encourage others with a warmth that fosters healing and hope. Though imperfectly practiced, it is when I both give and receive empathy, am loving and accepting of others, that I am most like Jesus. My heart feels lighter, and I am less concerned, more content in who I am and why I'm here.

"… 'Love the Lord your God with all your heart and with all your soul and with all your mind.' This is the first and greatest commandment. And the second is like it: 'Love your neighbor as yourself'" (Matthew 22: 37-39 NIV).

A round of golf with Kendra, another dear friend I have missed, was another time of restoration. The comfort of sitting side by side and catching up with each other's lives settled and nurtured me. The combination of sport, the warmth of the sun, and quality time with my friend refreshed and engaged me, mind, body and spirit: a gift and a reminder of the importance of nurturing all three. When my ball found the sand trap, it took me two swings to get out. I smiled and thought, how ironic. Had I practised this skill, it wouldn't intimidate me or throw me off my game. I wouldn't label my situation as desirable or undesirable. Instead, I would trust and rely on the skills mastered and confidently play from where I landed. The bumps, trips and dips into the valley, pothole, or sand trap don't have to result in a disaster. Sometimes the situation isn't that tricky or complicated, and sometimes there isn't a good choice available. Our most direct, desired route isn't always the safest, or possible one, and though detours are painful and disappointing, our course management skills gain insight and enable us to recover as we move through the hardship, obstacle, and/or trial.

Though I may struggle at times, I can take courage, I am never 'lost' or without hope. Always, a light shines: *"Your word a lamp to my feet and a light to my path"* (Psalm 119:105, ESV).

A crossroad lies just in front of me. One direction appears flat. The terrain is bland but unobtrusive, and if not exciting or rewarding, seemingly manageable. The other direction requires oxygen, climbing skills, like-minded others, and a shepherd who knows the way. Though daunting, and sure to bring times of pain and brokenness, it will be rewarding, nurturing and exhilarating as I ascend new heights of growth and freedom. Every day I wake up. I choose to take my next small step forward.

Epilogue

On July 20, 2021, there were zero active COVID-19 cases in Grande Prairie. One month later, there were 337, and the surrounding county had 122. On July 19 there were sixty-nine new cases in all of Alberta and just over one thousand active cases. On August 19, there are 817 new cases and 6,337 active cases. Again, though my journal has ended, COVID-19 has not.